# You Carried Me

# You Carried Me

*A Daughter's Memoir*

## Melissa Ohden

PLOUGH PUBLISHING HOUSE

Published by Plough Publishing House
Walden, New York
Robertsbridge, England
Elsmore, Australia
www.plough.com

ISBN: 978-0-87486-788-6
21 20 19 18 17     1 2 3 4 5 6

A catalog record for this book is available from the British Library.

Library of Congress Cataloging-in-Publication Data

Names: Ohden, Melissa, author.
Title: You carried me : a daughter's memoir / by Melissa Ohden.
Description: Walden, New York : Plough Publishing House, [2017]
Identifiers: LCCN 2016030873 (print) | LCCN 2016050913 (ebook) | ISBN
  9780874867886 (hardcover) | ISBN 9780874867893 (epub) | ISBN
9780874867916
  (pdf) | ISBN 9780874867909 ( mobi)
Subjects: LCSH: Abortion--Psychological aspects. |
Daughters--Psychological
  aspects. | Mother and child.
Classification: LCC HQ767 .O33 2017 (print) | LCC HQ767 (ebook) | DDC
  306.874/3--dc23
LC record available at https://lccn.loc.gov/2016030873

Printed in the United States of America

*To the woman who carried me,*
*and to Ron and Linda Cross, who carry me*
*in their hearts*

# One

*The tale of someone's life begins before they are born.*
— Michael Wood, *Shakespeare*

A THICK MANILA ENVELOPE arrived at my home in Sioux City with the afternoon mail one sunny day in May 2007. I knew without even looking at the return address that it came from the University of Iowa Hospitals in Iowa City and contained the medical records that would answer some of the questions I had been agonizing over most of my life.

Who am I? Where did I come from? Whose blood runs through my veins? And why was I given away? These are questions that most people who, like me, were adopted as infants want answered. But what I needed to know was more fundamental, and less innocent: Why did you try to kill me? And how is it possible that I survived?

I felt a clutch of panic in the pit of my stomach. Now that I had the information I had sought for so many years, my body, and spirit, rebelled. But as the Irish poet James Stephens – another adoptee – once wrote, "Curiosity will conquer fear even more than bravery will." So with trembling fingers, I peeled back the sealed flap of the envelope and faced the facts of my improbable life.

As I read through my tears the blandly rendered details of my narrow escape from death – "On August 24, saline infusion for abortion was done but was unsuccessful" – I discovered something I hadn't expected: the full names of my biological parents.

Their names were clearly written in the record of my birth, but I was left unnamed.

As I fought for my life in St. Luke's neonatal intensive care unit, it became clear to the doctors and nurses on hand that my birth mother had been pregnant for far longer than the eighteen to twenty weeks reported at the time of the abortion. The pediatrician who examined me a couple of days after I was delivered estimated that my gestational age at birth was about thirty-one weeks – well into the third trimester. The discrepancy hinted at something still unknown: How could any abortionist, much less one affiliated with one of the most prestigious hospitals in the region, have made such a mistake? What doctor or nurse would believe that a woman more than seven months pregnant was less than five months along?

Like other babies born prematurely, I had a host of serious medical problems including low birth weight (I weighed 2 pounds 14.5 ounces), jaundice, and respiratory distress. But my troubles were complicated by the after-effects of the poisonous saline solution I had endured in my mother's womb. No one knew the long-term consequences of surviving an abortion. Developmental delays are routine for preterm babies, but I also had seizures; and the list of potential complications grew to include mental retardation, blindness, and chronic poor health.

Three weeks after my birth I was transferred three hundred miles east, to the university hospital in Iowa

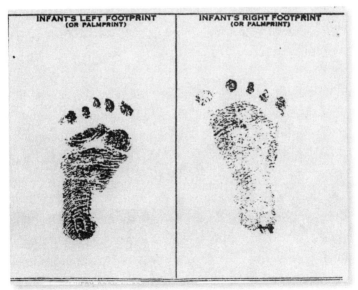

*Among the records I received were these prints of my feet.*

City. The nurses who cared for me, a nameless baby, made me tiny clothes and colorful booties. One nurse, Mary, decided I needed a name and dubbed me Katie Rose. For years after I left the NICU, my adoptive parents and Mary kept in touch, exchanging Christmas cards and letters with pictures of me and updates on my progress. When I got older, I wrote the letters myself; Mary and I began a friendship that would endure for decades. It made me feel so special that this nurse who had cared for me when no one else did still cared about me.

Meanwhile, the social services agency that had taken custody of me searched for a family willing to adopt a fragile newborn. This was no easy task because of my grim medical prognosis.

The search led to a small town, Curlew, Iowa, just one hundred miles from where I had been born. There a young couple who had adopted one child waited for another.

They were told that the baby would have needs that went far beyond food and shelter. Love they had in abundance; money for specialized medical care and services they did not. They drove five hours east to meet the tiny baby who needed a home. Unintimidated by the IV lines and the monitors attached to the skull of the baby whose head had been shaved from temple to temple, they made their choice. That's the day I first experienced a mother's love, in the arms of the woman who looked into my eyes and said, "You are mine."

Her name was Linda Cross, and although she wanted to bring me home right away, she had to wait another month to hold me in her arms again. In late October 1977, a social worker delivered all five pounds of me to the farmhouse Linda shared with her husband Ron and their four-year-old daughter Tammy. They named me Melissa Ann, after a friend who had become a quadriplegic after an accident. They admired her strength and her tenacious fight for life. They hoped for the same qualities in me.

Ron and Linda had grown up on the prairies of western Iowa. Palo Alto County had a population of about sixteen thousand people when they were born as part of the baby boom that followed the world war their fathers had fought in. They came from close families with deep roots. Ron was born in 1948 in Mallard, where four generations of his family had farmed the land for a hundred years. They grew corn and soybeans, and raised cattle and pigs. Linda was born a year later in Estherville, the seventh of nine children. Farming was part of her birthright as well: her father farmed and worked as an auto mechanic; her mom was a seamstress.

They met after they graduated from high school, at a drag race on the wide-open roads nearby. When I heard the story years later, it sounded like something straight out of the movie *Grease.* Fast cars, however, were the extent of their teenage rebellion. While their peers elsewhere in the country were engaging in the "summer of love," they carried on a traditional courtship in their Iowa hometowns. In April 1969, as their generation protested the Vietnam War and prepared to gather at the Woodstock Festival to celebrate sex, drugs, and rock-and-roll, they married in front of their families and friends at the Lutheran Church in Estherville, and began a life together.

At twenty years old, Ron was a tall, brawny young man, with a shock of light-brown hair and a smile that could light up a room. He had a perennial "farmer's tan" from driving around in his pickup truck or working the farm on his tractor. Linda was pretty and petite, with long blond hair and skin so fair she refused to wear shorts even on the hottest summer days because she was embarrassed by her too-white legs. Ron's gregarious personality was balanced by Linda's friendly but quiet demeanor. They were a perfect match.

The life they envisioned included children – lots of them. Their extended families included dozens of nieces and nephews, and they couldn't wait until their own children were part of the happy crowd of cousins. When a baby didn't come right away, they were patient; they enjoyed the time they had as newlyweds to get to know each other. But as the months turned to years they sought medical help and found that Linda suffered from a hormonal imbalance that made it very difficult for her to get pregnant. Surely they had their moments of regret as the years slipped by without the wished-for baby, but in Mom's words, "If you want a family, it doesn't matter how it's made." Three years after they married they took in their first foster children – two brothers who lived with them for nearly a year. They loved them deeply and were heartbroken when their mother reclaimed them. But that didn't stop them from opening their home and hearts to another little boy soon after, and when he was gone they took in a four-month-old baby girl with blond hair and blue eyes named Tammy, who became their beloved daughter.

It was into this happy home that I was welcomed after being released from the hospital. I was barely two months old.

I needed almost as much care at home as I had received in the NICU, but time, love, and attention cured most ills, and as I grew, I thrived. A year after I left the hospital, my adoption was finalized. As a small child I knew a few things for sure: My name was Missy Cross; I lived on a farm in Curlew, Iowa; I belonged to a family that included a mom, a dad, a big sister, and dozens of aunts, uncles, grandparents, and cousins.

And at some point before I can even remember I learned that I was doubly loved – by the parents who had chosen me as their own, and by a mother who had given birth to me and entrusted me to their care. That I was adopted was something I don't remember being told; it just *was* – a fact of life as ordinary as the sunshine in the morning, the starlight in the evenings, and the cozy walls around me.

In the 1970s and early 1980s there was a program on television that dramatized the *Little House on the Prairie* stories by Laura Ingalls Wilder. Tammy and I loved to watch that show, but truth be told, there wasn't much difference between the life lived by the Ingalls family in Walnut Grove, Minnesota, in the 1870s and the life we lived on the farm in Curlew a hundred years later. Sure, we had a lot more technology – like TV! But like the Ingalls family, we lived by the rhythm of the seasons.

In the summer we tended a large garden. Tammy and I had our own little plot that we sowed with seeds for flowers along with carrots, green beans, tomatoes, potatoes, and radishes. In the fall, we helped gather the vegetables that Mom would preserve for the winter. We had a collie named Laddie, whom we imagined to be the brother of the Lassie we saw on TV. He patiently submitted to being the playmate for two little girls, even letting us ride on his back. I'm not sure the cat I dressed up in doll clothes and pushed around in a stroller was quite as forgiving. But at least that was better than the treatment the cat got from our pet pig, whom we named Tailbiter because he liked to chew the cat's tail. When Dad would come in for lunch, he would always read a story to Tammy and me before he headed back out to the barn. Our life was defined by Dad's work on the farm, Mom's in the home, the help Tammy and I gave with the animals and the chores, and our membership in the close-knit community formed by our church and the dozens of relatives living nearby.

Mom loved to quilt and sew, and one of my earliest memories is running around with a gaggle of children while she worked with her friends on a quilting project. Kids were always a part of my parents' get-togethers; there was no separate "grown-up" time. My parents often gathered with their friends to play cards, and Tammy and I always were a part of the fun, running around with our playmates while our parents talked and played. Both Mom and Dad were good cooks, but I vividly remember the care Mom took to make snacks to share with their friends at these get-togethers. I watched her in awe, sure I could never make something so delicious out of the simple ingredients Mom gathered from the pantry.

The Methodist church where we worshipped was a second home. It was not just the place we went for prayer and spiritual nourishment; the church was also the center of our social life, the source of our friendships and fun. Tammy and I went to Sunday school, and Mom taught Vacation Bible School every year. The church organized outings that introduced us to the wider world. One of my earliest memories is going on a church trip to a place where we could swim in an indoor pool. Swimming inside – that seemed weird! We had a lot to learn.

The hard lessons began in 1982. Our farm, 160 acres, was rented from a large landowner. Mom and Dad were trying to save to buy their own land, but other priorities – like their daughters – always came first. When trouble hit, my parents had few resources to fall back on. They weren't the only ones. The combination of many factors – falling demand for agricultural exports, high levels of farm debt, rising interest rates, and reduced farm subsidies – created a nationwide farm crisis. We were among the victims.

As a five-year-old I was oblivious to the forces at play in the economy and the world. But I could sense the pain my mom and dad were feeling as our world was turned upside down. I vividly remember the day all our farm equipment and sows were auctioned. It was the first time I saw my parents cry. Tammy and I shared the grief we did not understand. We all knew that nothing would ever be the same.

To keep our family afloat, Dad moved to Storm Lake, a town about an hour's drive away, to take a job at a large hog slaughterhouse and meatpacking plant operated by Iowa Beef Processors (later Tyson Foods). Weekends meant driving back and forth to see him. It was a tense and lonely time for all of us.

A year or so after Dad started working in Storm Lake, Mom, Tammy, and I moved there to join him. We rented a small house on a quiet street that was home to many children and within walking distance of the school that Tammy and I started attending that September. I remember the relief I felt when we were all together again and the excitement of living in the "city" (population 8,800) and starting school as a first grader. That helped temper the sadness I felt over the biggest loss of all – our new landlord didn't allow pets, so Laddie had to stay in Curlew on the farm.

Our move to Storm Lake seemed to precipitate one momentous change after another. Money was in scarce supply, so Dad worked long hours at the packing plant, often taking on additional shifts at night and on weekends to earn overtime pay. Mom started to work a job away from home for the first time, as a bookkeeper at ALCO, a local department store. Her hours were often at night and on weekends too. One of our favorite times was when Dad would take Tammy and me to visit Mom at her office on Saturdays. We would meet her in the break room for lunch or a snack. Afterward, we would wander through the store, window-shopping. I remember looking longingly at the Cabbage Patch dolls in the toy department. I knew better than to ask; there wasn't any money for extras like that, and I didn't want Mom and Dad to feel bad about having to tell me no. I didn't have to say anything, though, for them to see how much I wanted a doll of my own – every little girl in America wanted one that year! When Christmas came, Santa left a Cabbage Patch doll under the tree. I named her Rachel, and still have her today. I knew how lucky I was to have that doll and was thankful.

And then in 1984, Mom gave birth to a son, Dustin. After fifteen years of marriage without any pregnancies, my mom hadn't even realized she was pregnant until she was twenty weeks along; before we knew it, Dustin was born, six weeks early. Mom and Dad told us about the baby a few days after my birthday. They found out she was pregnant on the day of my birthday party with neighborhood friends, and Mom told me later how hard it was for her to keep the news in until the party was over. When she and Dad finally burst out with it, I felt like the new baby was my birthday present! Just a few weeks later, Mom was ready to give birth. I remember staying with my grandparents while she was in the hospital; we played endless games of UNO to wile away the time. At last the call came – the baby was a boy!

To be a seven-year-old girl with her very own baby brother to care for was bliss. I couldn't quite understand why Mom and Dad would go to all the trouble of having a baby that way when they could just adopt one as they had Tammy and me, but I wasn't troubled by it. It never occurred to me that Dustin was somehow more theirs than I was. I don't think it ever occurred to them either.

As I got older, I took on more responsibilities in our home as Mom and Dad worked to provide for our family's simple needs. Tammy and I walked the few blocks to and from school with our neighborhood friends. We were latchkey kids who came home after school to fend for ourselves. Sometimes our neighbors Myron and Dorothy, who lived in a pretty white house on the corner, would keep an eye on us for Mom and Dad. One of their daughters, Lynn, was in high school. Tammy and I idolized her and wanted to be just like her when we got older – she was so cool. I remember how Tammy and I would argue over doing the dishes – neither one of us wanted to be the one who had to dry! But despite that daily tug-of-war, I loved helping out at home and learning to cook – now I could prepare some of the dishes I had seen Mom make when we lived on the farm. I especially loved watching over Dustin. We nicknamed him "Dennis the Menace" because of his blond hair and bright blue eyes, but he wasn't a menace at all – just a happy little boy. When I got older I began to feel burdened by all the extra responsibility, but at that time, it just made me happy to know that my parents trusted and relied on me. Even so, I dreaded the days when there was no school and my parents had to work. I missed them, especially my Mom, something awful.

The learning difficulties the doctors had prepared my parents for never developed; I excelled at school and my parents and teachers fed my intellectual and artistic curiosity with books and music. I wore out my library card at the Storm Lake Public Library, and beginning in fourth grade my teachers challenged me by placing me in classes for gifted students. Shel Silverstein's *A Light in the Attic* launched my lifelong love of poetry, and Beverly Cleary's books were my favorite fiction. I remember feeling a little bit like Ramona, with Tammy as big sister Beezus. Reading *Ramona and Her Father* helped me understand a little more about our family's financial struggles. Money was always scarce, but good report cards were rewarded with a little gift or a special dinner out. Mom and Dad were determined that Tammy, Dustin, and I would be the first in our family to earn bachelor's degrees.

Dustin's birth sparked my natural curiosity about my own life story. I knew, of course, that most babies were not given up for adoption but raised by their biological mothers and fathers. Who were mine? My parents let me look at the file about my adoption, which included information about the background of my birth family. I learned that my birth parents had been college students; that they were both athletic and that my birth mother and her family were musically inclined. I enjoyed sports and music, too, and it made me happy to think that in a way I was like them. I was *sure* I looked like my birth mother, just as Dustin looked like Mom. I wasn't motivated by any sense of discontent; quite the opposite. Just as the birth of a little brother had added to the love in our home, not divided it, I felt knowing about my birth family would enrich my life with more people to love.

Our move to Storm Lake brought changes, many of them good. But the biggest loss, apart from the time my parents had to spend away from home, was that church was no longer a home away from home. We were members of the United Methodist Church, and Mom and Dad tried to make sure Tammy, Dustin, and I went even when they could not, but church was no longer the focal point of our lives. Still, my faith remained strong. Soon it would be tested by fire.

# Two

*Three things cannot long stay hidden:*
*the sun, the moon, and the truth.*
— Buddha

O<small>NE DAY WHEN I WAS</small> about eight years old, my mom, dad, and I were sitting in the kitchen of close family friends, visiting. The two men had worked together on the farm and had many things to talk about. I sat quietly, listening avidly as I always did to grown-up conversation, hoping to pick up the secret code of adulthood. Our friends' son Billy was there too, and all of a sudden he looked at Dad and me and said, in a tone of unexpected discovery, "I never noticed it before, but you two have the same eyes!"

Now, Billy knew I was adopted; he also could see that my eyes and my dad's are nothing alike – his are light blue, mine are green. But perhaps Billy perceived something deeper. Love had made us father and daughter; we looked to the world like we belonged together.

Yet there was no hiding the fact that when it came to the Cross family, in the words of the old *Sesame Street* song, "One of these . . . is not like the others." Mom, Dad, Tammy, and Dustin were blond; my hair was black. They all had blue or brown eyes; mine are green. My olive skin tone stood out against their pale white skin. I looked very different.

With my sister Tammy, the differences went far deeper than appearance. We diverged in temperament, talents, and interests. I loved school; she hated it. I was controlled; she was spontaneous. I was a glass-half-full person; she had the opposite outlook. As we got older, the tight bonds formed during our happy childhood on the farm began to fray. Still, our lives centered on our home, and we were happy sharing it with Mom, Dad, Dustin, and each other.

When I was in seventh grade, we moved to a new house. For the first time in their lives, Mom and Dad were homeowners! The American dream to own a home and the land it stands on had eluded them on the farm; finally it had come true. The new house firmly planted our roots in Storm Lake, and we embraced all the wonderful things the community had to offer. The town's Fourth of July celebration was a highlight of the year. Summers were spent in and around the lake, boating, hanging out on the beach, rollerblading with my friends. I still had happy memories of the farm, but Storm Lake was home.

Dad planted a garden with flowers and vegetables at the new house, and I worked alongside him. We both loved the outdoors and would often take long walks together around the lake on the weekends. My parents had a huge, old-fashioned record player and hundreds of albums. Tammy, Dustin, and I would have "dance parties" in the living room while my parents listened to their old records. Dad had a beautiful voice. Back in Curlew he had sung in the church choir, but in Storm Lake he sang only to entertain us. I loved to sing, too, and would join him. Years later, we sang together at a wedding or two.

Mom now worked at the bank, and although our neighborhood was close to her office and near Tammy's high school, it was across town from the junior high I attended and Dustin's daycare. Early each morning Dad would drop Dustin and me off at our Uncle Reg and Aunt Deb's home next to the school before going to work. We would stay there until it was time for classes to begin and Dustin's daycare to open. If Mom and Dad had to go to work early, I would walk, pushing Dustin in the stroller. I would pick him up after school and head home. Often he would fall asleep before Mom and Dad got home from work.

We appreciated our new home all the more because we had shared in the sacrifices that made it possible. Mom and Dad both worked so hard, in jobs that kept them away from home for long hours. They never were without work, but some years their income was so low that we qualified for free lunches at school. Their jobs kept them from attending many of my school activities: concerts, plays, and athletic events. When I was in the eighth grade I made the Northwest Iowa Honor Choir. I was so proud! The day of the concert, I had to meet the other students and teachers at a café downtown. Neither Mom nor Dad could give me a ride, so I had to walk in the cold November drizzle. By the time I arrived, my hair was a frizzy mess and I looked and felt terrible. I was so embarrassed and frustrated that my parents weren't able to give me a ride like the other parents. I never told them how I felt, though. I knew it was tough for them not to be able to provide us with the things other town kids took for granted.

I was anxious to start earning money for myself. I started out as a babysitter for kids in the neighborhood, but got my first "real" job, bussing tables at a local restaurant, when I was just thirteen. Work was a fact of life for me: Mom and Dad provided for our basic needs, but if I wanted to buy a new dress for homecoming, or go to a movie or to the latest Boyz II Men concert, I had to earn the money.

The job at the restaurant was the first of many I would have as a teenager, including a stint at the Hy-Vee grocery store, followed by several years in the store's floral department. Working there taught me a lot about self-discipline and sacrifice; the long hours on the job for proms, Mother's Day, and Valentine's Day sometimes made it hard to truly celebrate those occasions myself. Still, I loved learning about all the different varieties of flowers and plants, creating arrangements, getting to know the customers, and forming a close relationship with my coworkers and boss. I liked to think about who was going to receive the flowers, and why. A dozen roses – romance? A mixed arrangement – a new baby? A flowering plant – a get-well wish? My work there helped me learn about people in ways that I didn't expect, and I saw that I was privileged to participate in a small way in their joys and sorrows.

In the flower shop I was surrounded by beauty, something that at times seemed in scarce supply. At fourteen, my eyes were opening to the wider world, and I didn't like much of what I saw. I watched the news on TV and occasionally read the newspaper. Every day it seemed like there was another story about a woman being victimized: Jaycee Lee Dugard was abducted in California; dozens of women were sexually assaulted and harassed by members of the military in the Tailhook scandal in Las Vegas; Miss Black Rhode Island was raped by boxing champ Mike Tyson in Indiana. I learned that women and girls close to home could be victims, too, of domestic violence and sexual assault, and of subtler forms of abuse, in the workplace and at home.

I was determined not to be a victim! Our family wasn't one of those that talked about current events at the dinner table each night; I don't think my parents ever participated in the presidential caucuses that drew the attention of the world to Iowa every four years. But I came to see political activism as one way to fight for equal rights, wages, and opportunities for women. I admired President George H. W. Bush, but I identified with Hillary Clinton's unapologetic feminism – I too wanted to do more with my life than "stay home and bake cookies."

By the time I started eighth grade at Storm Lake Junior High in September 1991, the gulf between Tammy and me had grown to the size of an ocean. She was a high school junior that year – a girl in a hurry, straining for the independence and privileges of adulthood. She had a boyfriend, an older guy who went to college nearby, and she began to spend more time at his apartment than she did at home.

Mom and Dad didn't talk about it much, but I could see they were worried about her. One day while Mom was working a second job at the Storm Lake Walmart, a coworker – the mother of one of Tammy's good friends – pulled her aside into an empty room in the receiving area to tell her something that confirmed her worst fears. Tammy was pregnant.

Mom told Dad the news that evening, and soon I knew too. My parents were disappointed; that was clear to see. But there wasn't a trace of anger in their response to Tammy's pregnancy. There was, however, a sense of urgent concern about what would happen next.

Would Tammy keep the baby? Would she give it up for adoption, as her own birth mother had given her up? Or would she make the choice that so many others in the same situation had made, and end the life growing within her?

There was no question in our home where Mom and Dad came down on that: their convictions, formed by their faith and their own experiences, were firmly on the side of life. They made it clear that they would do everything in their power to help Tammy raise her baby, or would help find a loving adoptive home if that was what she wanted. What they wouldn't do – couldn't do – was support an abortion.

But Tammy made her own decisions – her pregnancy was vivid proof of that. Emotions were running high, and during one explosive conversation Mom and Dad were desperate for Tammy to see that every choice – even one that seems easy and simple, one that would just make the whole "problem" go away – has a consequence, and that every life, no matter how inconvenient, has a purpose. So, I later learned, they told her a long-held secret about her own sister, and she was convinced.

I was excited and happy when I learned that Tammy would keep her baby and raise him with our family's help. I was thrilled with the idea of becoming an aunt. Never would I have guessed the role my own life story had played in her decision.

I found out soon enough, though, in a way that rattled me to the core. Tammy's pregnancy hadn't brought us closer together; if anything, we were further apart than ever. Our relationship was one of mutual disregard, punctuated by passionate fights that betrayed an anger out of proportion to the trivial matters at hand.

It was in the midst of one of those fights that Tammy blurted out the words that would change my life forever.

"At least my parents wanted me!"

"What's that supposed to mean?" I replied. Both of our birth mothers had wanted us – that's how we came to be adopted! I couldn't figure out what she was talking about. It was just Tammy spouting off.

But as I turned to face her, I saw that it was much more than that. The look of compassion and sisterly affection on her face at that moment was something I hadn't seen in a long time.

"You don't know? You really don't know, do you?" she said.

I stared at her in confusion. "Know what? What are you talking about?"

Tammy's face crumpled; it looked like a balloon after it pops. Quietly she said, "Wait for Mom and Dad to come home. Ask them, and you will see."

And so I waited.

Mom was the first one home. It was already dark when I met her at the door. The words spilled out of me as I told her about my fight with Tammy, and what she had said. My biggest worry was that I would be scolded for arguing with my sister; I was completely unprepared for what came next.

Mom and I made our way into the dimly lit living room. We sat knee-to-knee, Mom on the sofa, me on the adjacent love seat.

Mom's voice was soft and low as she took my hands in hers. "We never meant to keep this from you. . . . We should have told you when we told Tammy, but there was just no easy way. . . . We love you, honey, we'll always love you. . . ." She paused and took a deep breath. "Missy, your birth mother had an abortion during her pregnancy with you and you survived."

I sat for a moment in utter disbelief—how was this even possible? And then I fell into my mom's arms and sobbed.

My tears gave way to questions, but Mom had very few answers. She knew only the barest outline: she'd been told that my birth mother had an abortion at St. Luke's Hospital in Sioux City and that my body had been laid aside on the assumption that I was dead or dying, but a nurse heard me whimper, realized I was alive, and saved my life. Those facts didn't satisfy; I wanted to know why, not how! Still, we talked through the night, holding on to each other, speaking secret words of love and understanding. I had always been a daddy's girl, but that night I clung to my mom, and the closeness we felt on that momentous night endures to this day.

Finally, exhaustion overtook me and I slept. The next day was a Saturday. Dad was home when I came downstairs for breakfast. He looked up from his coffee as I walked into the kitchen. I could see he was struggling.

He and Mom had helped one daughter choose life by telling her the truth about my birth; why did the price have to be paid in my tears and heartache? I took a lot of comfort from his embrace, but as his emotions threatened to overwhelm both him and me, I put on a brave face and found myself comforting him. "I'm OK, Dad, really I am."

But I wasn't. In my mind I understood why my parents had not told me the truth – how could a child be expected to understand something like that? But in my heart I felt a deep sense of betrayal. I had been deceived about my own identity. Even Tammy knew who I was before I did! They had no right! I felt like the life I had been living was a lie; I had to go back to the beginning and reconstruct it in all its painful truth. That included facing the only conclusion I could draw from the fact of my survival – that the people who had conceived me had also tried to destroy me.

In the days that followed I began the long and painful work of processing this new reality. I confided first in one of my best friends, Kendra, who listened with a loving heart on that Saturday after I first found out, and many other days besides. She remembers how upset I was, not just by *what* I had learned about myself, but by *how* I had learned it. As we stood on the threshold of our own adolescence, she helped me process and confront adult-sized crises far beyond anything either of us could comprehend.

Mom was my strength and my comfort. One day she gave me an article she had clipped from a newspaper years before. Titled "Diary of an Unborn Child," it chronicles the life of a baby girl from the moment of conception through the early stages of development – when her heart starts to beat, her fingernails begin to form, her hair starts to grow – and imagines the baby's dialogue with her mother until the day her life is ended by abortion. I read it over until I knew it by heart. Each time I got to the words "Today my mother aborted me," a raging anger welled up inside. I had wanted to be a champion for women who were victimized, yet here I was, a victim myself!

I didn't know what to do with all that anger; it wouldn't be long before I turned it inward. But in the early days, as I struggled to understand what couldn't be understood, I turned to things I loved – nature, books, music. I would walk the several miles to the lake just to sit and watch the waves. I would listen to instrumental music on my Walkman – lyrics seemed like too much of an intrusion into my own thoughts, but the rhythms of the Native American music I had started listening to – probably after I saw the movie *Dances with Wolves* – calmed me.

Most of all, though, I sought solace in my faith; the church that had become such a marginal part of my life since moving to Storm Lake became central once again. I was about to be confirmed in the United Methodist Church, and although Pastor Shaw hadn't been able to offer me much insight when I shared my story – he had looked like a deer caught in the headlights when I told him – I found in the Bible the words that would sustain me.

There were about fifteen young men and women in my confirmation class, and we met every Sunday night for about nine months from the fall of 1991 until the spring of 1992. When we were confirmed, we each were given a cake inscribed with a verse we had chosen from scripture. Most of the other students chose the words of John: "For God so loved the world that he gave his only Son, that whoever believes in him shall not perish but have eternal life." For my verse, though, I reached back to the "weeping prophet" from the Old Testament, Jeremiah: "Before I formed you in the womb, I knew you; before you were born, I set you apart."

# Three

*He knew that there was no quick comfort for emotions*
*like those. They were deeper and they did not*
*need to be told. They were felt.*
— Lois Lowry, *The Giver*

TAMMY'S SON MICHAEL was born in the summer of 1992, a beautiful baby with bright blue eyes and hair so blond it almost looked white. Tammy and Michael lived with us, and although his father was part of the picture at first, his presence faded as he and Tammy drifted apart. It was hard to see her shoulder the responsibility of being a single teenage mother. Only after I became a mother myself could I fully appreciate the sacrifices she made. In an instant her life had changed from being a carefree teenager to a mother whose son depended on her for everything. Many mornings she went off to school after a sleepless night caring for Michael; she squeezed in her homework around her baby's schedule, and her social life ground to a halt. Mom, Dad, and I would help out when we could, but the burden was undeniably Tammy's.

Michael's birth didn't erase the conflicts between us, but it did engender in me a deep respect for her decision to raise him. What made that possible was the steadfast support of our parents, who provided resources, stability, and unconditional love. I remember so clearly the day he was born; every one of us fell head over heels for him. Michael's birth brought so much joy to our family; it brought us all together around a shared purpose – the well-being of this precious child.

Yet for me, there was a deeper wound that could not be healed by this baby's birth. Mom and Dad's support for Tammy and her decision to be a mother to Michael had changed his destiny. I began to wonder if someone could have changed my birth mother's and mine. Had she even told her parents that she was pregnant? Did they know she had an abortion? I tried to imagine my birth mother in Tammy's position. What if she had wanted to have me and raise me as her own, but didn't have anyone to turn to for help? I could see how hard it was for Tammy – and she had the support of her whole family! What if my birth mother's family had rejected or abandoned her? If they had given her the support Mom and Dad gave so freely to Tammy, would I have been aborted?

My August birthday, the first since learning the truth, didn't seem any cause for celebration. Tammy was four years older than me, but her birth date was the day before mine. On her birthday, she made plans with friends and had a fun night out. In contrast, I felt like I would never have a happy birthday again. The image I'd had in earlier years of being born to a woman who loved me and wanted me, but had selflessly given me away so I could have a better life, now seemed a sick fantasy. I was still on summer vacation; Mom and Dad were working as usual, and I was alone. I avoided my friends' calls and wallowed in my misery. Mom had an inkling of the struggle I was trying to hide; for the first and only time in my life she gave me her credit card and urged me to spend the day shopping for something I really wanted.

What I really wanted? The only thing I truly wanted – needed – was for the oppressive weight that had been loaded on me to be lifted. No day at the mall or lame birthday "celebration" could do that.

And so, as I turned fifteen, I began my double life.

As I entered high school that September, I seemed to have it all together. I had lots of girlfriends, was doing well academically, and participated in speech and drama after school. My favorite subject was English, mainly because I loved to read and write. I really liked participating in speech and debate competitions, mostly because of the feeling of camaraderie that came from being part of a team.

I met my first boyfriend in ninth grade when we boarded the bus to a Special Olympics competition at the same time. I was there as a volunteer; Chad was there to support his sister, who had special needs. I was so impressed by how tenderly he cared for her. Chad played basketball and many of our dates involved me watching him play.

But I spent most of my time with my girlfriends. Natalie, Kendra, and I would go out to the movies and have sleepovers at each other's homes, and we made sure to attend the games of our school's football and basketball teams. With my friend Holly I would go to dances and hang out around town. After we got our licenses, we would drive around for hours, singing along to the radio and talking about everything.

Life at home settled into a new normal. I helped care for Michael, as I had with Dustin. Some people around town thought he was mine because we were together so often. His babysitter's house was right by our high school – Tammy was a senior that year – and we would walk him there in the morning on our way to classes. Tammy struggled with so many things that year; she didn't hesitate to take out her stress on me. Even so, she knew she could count on me to help her. It wasn't unusual for her to poke her head into my classroom at the end of the day and ask me to pick Michael up for her on the way home.

To my teachers, friends, coworkers at the flower shop, and siblings I seemed happy, healthy, hardworking, and well liked. To my parents, I was the perfect child – responsible, obedient, successful. They were amazed and relieved by how well I had handled the terrible truth they had shared with me. Both Tammy and Dustin had strong opinions and didn't hesitate to share them – when they were unhappy, everyone knew it! I was more of a people-pleaser – my top priority was to keep everyone happy, even if it meant making myself miserable. They didn't see – I didn't allow them to see – that I was falling apart.

I began to spend large amounts of time alone, brooding in my bedroom. My obsessive and distorted thoughts about my birth overwhelmed me. Looking back now, with the benefit of the professional experience I would gain much later, I can see that I was experiencing a post-traumatic stress reaction, plus a kind of survivor's guilt about living when so many others had died through abortion. Back then, all I knew was what I felt: I am not OK; something is wrong with me; I am not loved.

The burden was so heavy, I despaired of ever being free of it. So I lifted the only weight I could: I starved myself. In some strange, twisted way, it gave me a feeling of power at a time when I felt most powerless. I couldn't escape my feelings, or change the circumstances of my birth, but I could control what I ate.

I was good at hiding things, and I hid this well. My parents left early for work; they didn't see that I skipped breakfast and didn't bring a lunch to school. In the evenings, if they got home early enough, we would have dinner as a family. I ate just enough to avoid their notice. I exulted in the feeling of power and reveled in my secret victories. The weight began to fall off. I was slender to begin with; soon, I thought, I might just disappear. I took perverse pleasure in that idea.

I knew I was flirting with disaster, but believed I was in control – even of my anorexia. I was aware of other girls at school who had crossed the line into bulimia; I thought they were nuts! I knew I would *never* stick my finger down my throat to force myself to vomit.

Until I did. By now I was sixteen. I was still presenting a picture-perfect façade to the world. I had saved most of the money I earned from my job, so soon after getting my driver's license I was able with Mom and Dad's help to buy my first car – a red Chevy Beretta. They got me started, but I had to keep up with the payments myself. Looking back now, I am amazed that they trusted me enough to let me own a car. I loved the freedom that came with having a car of my own! No more long trudges to and from school, and no waiting for Mom or Dad to get home to give me a ride to the basketball game or a friend's party.

But my inner pain was the real driving force in my life. It threatened to consume me, and so it seemed almost logical that I should get rid of it by expelling it from my body by force. Almost daily, I would lean over the toilet, throw up, look at the vomit, and say to myself, "Huh – that's what my pain looks like."

Bulimia gave me a sense of control as exhilarating as it was self-destructive, but it wasn't enough. Many teenagers drank alcohol when I was in high school, and I was no exception. I got my first taste at my friend Kendra's house, one night when her parents were out. We found a bottle of peppermint schnapps, and in our ignorance we drank it by the glassfull, not realizing how potent it was. Soon we were passed out on the floor. When Kendra's parents got home hours later, we jumped up to greet them and one of us – we were so loaded we still disagree who – walked right into the wall!

That incident got us both grounded for a while, but drinking was soon an ordinary part of my life, as it was for almost every teenager in town.

The drinking age was twenty-one, but that was no deterrent. Older friends would buy us whatever we wanted at the liquor store. I found that getting drunk temporarily eased the pain I carried inside. It lowered my inhibitions and dulled my memories. When I was drinking, I didn't have to be the responsible one, the overachiever, the perfect child. I could just be . . . me, with all my pain and confusion. Most of the kids I hung around with drank at parties on weekends, and I did too, but I was probably the only one to keep a bottle of vodka in my bedroom closet and another under the back seat of my car. I did not open them – I never drank alone – but in a strange way it comforted me to know that drinking myself to oblivion was always an option.

I couldn't escape knowing the consequences of pre-
marital sex; Tammy's son slept each night in the room
next to mine. That didn't stop me from becoming sexually active. Since my innocent and well-chaperoned
courtship with Chad in ninth grade, I almost always
had a boyfriend. By the time I was in tenth grade, those
relationships were far from innocent. Alcohol definitely
eased the way. I was deathly afraid of ending up like
Tammy, or worse, like my own birth mother, who I knew
from my adoption records had been pregnant with me
at nineteen. I was vigilant about protecting myself from
pregnancy, but I was reckless with my body and my heart.
I found myself attracted to older guys from around town
and gave myself to them freely, naively expecting love in
return. There's a song by the band Cheap Trick that was
released around the time I was born; its verse seemed to
express what I wanted:

> I want you to want me
> I need you to need me
> I'd love you to love me . . .

But the chorus captured what was going on beneath the
surface:

> Feeling all alone without a friend,
>     you know you feel like dying
> Oh, didn't I, didn't I, didn't I see you crying?

Bulimia, alcohol, sex – these were my unholy trinity of
coping mechanisms. They dulled, but didn't deaden, my

torment. That all this suffering was hidden from everyone who knew me seemed to be the point – I was singularly chosen for misery; I was different, broken, unworthy. Alone.

Soon after I learned I was an abortion survivor, I started to speak about it openly to my classmates. Back in eighth grade, my English teacher encouraged me to talk to the class about what had happened to me. I set the room up so there was one empty chair in the front row, representing how our class would have looked had my mother's abortion succeeded. Many years later, Kendra told me how affected she was by that speech – "I remember being proud of you, confused, and just amazed that something like that could happen," she wrote. Later, during a speech and debate competition, I spoke about the issue of abortion and my own story. It was during a regional competition, and even though I was too sick to ride the bus – I had strep throat and mono – I begged Mom to drive me to Sioux City so I could participate. I received high marks but the judges didn't advance me to the next level of the competition. I always wondered whether my topic had something to do with that.

Speaking about my past was therapeutic at first, but as I got older it became another source of isolation. Girls I knew at school got pregnant; one of my schoolmates had a miscarriage; others had abortions or kept their babies. Almost everyone at school knew about these things; we lived in a small community and gossip spread fast. Yet no one would speak about them to me. Sometimes the motive was compassion; other times it was shame or self-justification. It didn't matter to me what the motive was – all I knew was that I felt like a freak.

I began to have nightmares almost every night. One of the most frightening was a dream of being in a car that I couldn't navigate or control. The car would careen through twists and turns on a dark road; I couldn't see what was ahead and was powerless to steer or stop. The dream inevitably ended with a crash. To stave off the sleep I dreaded, I would read and write poetry. I tore up most of my poems as soon as I wrote them; I couldn't bear to keep tangible evidence of my anguish and confusion. But I kept this one by Emily Dickinson; it helped me to know that someone else had felt what I was feeling.

> Pain has an element of blank;
> It cannot recollect
> When it began, or if there were
> A day when it was not.
>
> It has no future but itself,
> Its infinite realms contain
> Its past, enlightened to perceive
> New periods of pain.

The great American poet Robert Frost once said, "A poem begins as a lump in the throat, a sense of wrong, a homesickness, a lovesickness. . . . An emotion finds the thought and the thought finds the words." To find the words to write, I first had to find the thoughts. That exercise in self-reflection, over a period of many months, helped me understand that what I was doing was intensifying my pain, not alleviating it. I wanted to be rid of the pain! At long last my heart and mind turned to the One from whom I could not hide my inner life and my secret sins – the One who alone had the power to set me free.

After confirmation, I went to church only sporadically. I didn't see why I needed to go to church to have a relationship with God. My parents didn't insist that I go; often they couldn't go themselves. When I finally turned to God I would repeat the Our Father over and over again until I fell asleep. In time I began to ask for forgiveness for what I had been doing, and to beg for a sense of direction. Maybe I was driven more by fear of his justice than I was drawn by his mercy. But most of all, I was homesick for the perfect love that I desperately wanted to believe in.

I began to cling to Jesus in prayer, and as I did, I felt the guilt and shame and self-loathing that had defined me for so long begin to slip away. I still felt deeply damaged, though, like the psalmist who wrote, "I know my transgressions; my sin is ever before me" (Psalm 51). Slowly, with God's grace, I was able to turn my gaze from my inward pain and look anew on the world around me.

I had started volunteering as a mentor in a third-grade classroom, working with children who needed tutoring, often because their families had recently come to the United States and English was not their native language.

In my senior year, one of the little boys from that class came to an assembly at the high school and gave me and the other volunteers flowers to thank us for our help. I was so touched by that gesture. That experience gave me my first real sense of satisfaction and joy from serving others.

I had always been an avid reader; now, as I groped my way through the fog of pain, I found myself drawn to biographies. Learning about the lives of great heroes and ordinary people gave me inspiration, strength, and most of all a greater understanding of how suffering could give way to peace. I read Nelson Mandela's autobiography, *Long Walk to Freedom,* and was in awe of what he had endured and overcome, and his ability to forgive those who had persecuted him. I read *The Color Purple* and was also touched by Alice Walker's personal story. She had an abortion while she was in college, and the volume of poems she wrote to help her come to terms with the grief and depression she felt in the aftermath was her first published work. I didn't agree with everything she believed, including her continued support for abortion, but this insight resonated with me deeply: "How simple a thing it seems to me," she wrote, "that to know ourselves as we are, we must know our mothers' names."

I watched *Schindler's List* when it came out in 1993. I remember walking out of the theater in absolute silence, stunned by what I had witnessed. I was deeply moved by the footage of Jewish people, who had been saved from death by Oskar Schindler, putting flowers on his grave in Jerusalem. I still remember the Talmudic inscription on the ring given Schindler by the workers in his factory: "Whoever saves one life saves the world entire." Who had saved my life, I wondered, on the day I'd entered the world?

*The Giver,* by Lois Lowry, was published when I was in high school. It's still one of my favorite books. Reading it helped me understand that the ability to feel pain and suffer is part of what makes us human beings able to give and receive love. Central to the story is the moment when Jonas sees his father, who had seemed to him a good man, "release" a newborn identical twin from life by giving him a lethal injection. Twins were seen as an aberration that violated the "sameness" and "climate control" humans had enforced to blot out memories of pain and hardship. The smaller twin is killed without remorse or question, and disposed of as if he were trash. It didn't take much for me to see the parallels to my own life, and the lives of so many others who had been disposed of through abortion.

As I approached my high school graduation in 1996, I was finally feeling OK again about myself and my future. I no longer felt a need to self-destruct through bulimia. I rarely drank and threw away the unopened stash of liquor in my room and car. I developed a relationship with a steady boyfriend. I felt freer to talk about who I was and what had happened to me with my friends and new people I met. I was on my way to integrating my past into a larger life story, one I couldn't wait to write.

One evening while flipping channels on the television set in our living room, I stumbled across a rerun of *The Maury Povich Show*. What I saw and heard knocked the breath out of me: on the show that day was a fourteen-year-old girl, Gianna Jessen, who had recently been told by her adoptive mother that she had been born to a seventeen-year-old unwed mother after a failed abortion attempt. I'll never forget her words: "It's not that I'm mad at my birth mother at all. I forgive her totally for what she did. . . . This is what God has given me. I don't feel bad about it; I'm just happy. . . ."

If she could feel that way, maybe I could too.

# Four

*We must travel in the direction of our fear.*
— John Berryman, from "A Point of Age"

$B$Y THE TIME I GRADUATED from Storm Lake High in May 1996, I was happy. My grades put me near the top of my class and I was selected as a member of the National Honor Society. I had big ambitions – I wanted to change the world from the top down, and envisioned a future in Washington, DC, working in politics or law. I had it all planned out – right down to the nanny and cook I would employ while I worked in a high-powered law firm! I had briefly considered a career in social work after attending a Career Day at my high school, but concluded that I could never work in a field that offered so little money and so much heartache.

But first I had to earn a degree. The college catalogs that flooded our mailbox offered a world of possibilities.

Mom and Dad encouraged me to think big, but even though I dreamed of one day heading east to DC, I limited my search to schools within a few hours' drive from home. I was admitted to several colleges in Iowa and nearby states, and decided to go for my first choice, the University of South Dakota, where I had been accepted as an honors student in political science.

Everything about USD appealed to me. The beautiful campus had a mix of historic buildings dating to the school's founding in the 1880s, as well as modern facilities. Vermillion was a charming college town just a few miles west of the Iowa border. USD had an excellent academic reputation and the political science department was highly respected. I couldn't wait to get started.

Mom and Dad helped me pack up my car for the drive to campus for orientation in August. I had my comforter and pillows, my clothes, my stereo and Alanis Morissette CDs, a microwave and a television set for my dorm room. One thing I didn't have was my adoption file, which included the descriptions of my birth parents and their families. I had stored it in a little treasure trunk, decorated with pictures of kittens, that I kept in my bedroom closet; but when it came time to sort through my belongings to decide what to take with me to South Dakota, I discovered the papers were missing. I didn't worry about where they could have gone. I had pored over them so intently that I knew their contents by heart.

I was filled with confidence in myself and my future that summer. I was on the verge of my nineteenth birthday. For so long I had dreaded reaching the age at which my birth mother had been pregnant with me. Now as I approached that milestone, it seemed a welcome step forward and once again a cause for celebration.

My roommate at USD was Heidi, one of my best friends from home. She was one of several kids from Storm Lake who were on campus, as freshmen or upperclassmen. She and I settled into our dorm room and got to know the other girls on our hall. Conversations naturally turned to our backgrounds – where did we grow up? What were our parents like? Did we have any brothers and sisters?

It was in those interactions with my peers that I got my first real taste of being silenced.

The first days at college are intense; total strangers become intimate friends in a matter of days. Secrets are spilled and souls are bared without reserve. In that context I opened up about the fact that I was a survivor of a legal abortion. In the midst of conversations about every kind of abuse, abandonment, and human heartache, I learned quickly that my story was one that could not be heard, and therefore must not be told. Abortion-on-demand was the holy grail of the feminist ideology my classmates adhered to; anything that challenged its essential rightness must be suppressed. I too considered myself an ardent supporter of women's rights, but I learned there was no place in the feminist fold for women who object to the procedure that had nearly ended my life before it began.

The icy chill with which my story was met the few times I shared it stirred up the familiar feelings of shame and fear I had faced in high school. My classmates' rejection hurt me in a very deep place. Once again I was made to feel like a freak. How I longed to run home for a good cry; here at school, the only place you could be alone was the bathroom! Why could I never be accepted like everyone else?

I kept up with my classes and went through the motions of a social life, but as the semester wore on, I felt isolated and oppressed by a dread that I could not name. I was homesick and depressed, and the nightmares that had once plagued me returned in full force. Mom had a sense from our phone calls that something was wrong, but I didn't tell anyone how miserable I felt. The moment finals were over in December, I packed my belongings and drove home to Storm Lake through a raging blizzard. I didn't go back.

Many years later, I learned that another nineteen-year-old girl at the University of South Dakota had endured a difficult freshman year in Vermillion. That girl was my birth mother, who had been secretly pregnant with me for most of her spring semester there. I may even have been conceived on campus. Could my feelings of unease and anxiety at USD have been rooted in some primal way in that experience? Had my mother hidden her tears in the very corners where I tried to hide mine?

Of course, my birth mother was long gone from USD by the time I arrived there in 1996. But someone close to her – who, I later discovered, had played a decisive role in my fate – was right there on campus during my horrible fall semester. My birth mother's mother – my grandmother – was a professor at the university's College of Nursing. I had no inkling of her presence at the time. Did she know about me? If so, what were her feelings about me, her granddaughter? Did we ever cross paths and unwittingly look each other in the eye?

๑

Back home, life settled into a new routine. I enrolled at Buena Vista University, which was located in Storm Lake. I probably should have considered it more seriously when I first looked at colleges, but at the time the lure of going away for college blinded me to the fact that it, too, had an excellent reputation and offered a great education. It turned out to be the perfect school for me. I started working again at the flower shop at Hy-Vee grocery store, and went out with my longtime boyfriend, who was still in Storm Lake. I lived at home with Mom, Dad, and Dustin: Tammy and Michael lived nearby in their own apartment. My parents may have wondered about my unhappy experience at USD, but they gave me the freedom and space I needed to find a new path forward.

One of the casualties of my experience at USD was my desire to make a career in politics. My encounter with the political correctness surrounding the abortion issue had left me jaded and wary; my early idealism and passion had given way to indifference. I had never even taken a political science course at USD, because I had filled my first semester schedule with core courses I had wanted to get out of the way. Now my interest turned to one of my first loves – literature.

I chose a dual major in English and education, and resolved to share my enthusiasm for reading with young people. I was inspired by the example of one of my high school English teachers, who had helped a bunch of small-town kids experience the great books of English literature. Somehow she had made the remote Yorkshire moorland, home to a brooding Heathcliff in love with the unattainable Cathy, come alive in the prairies of western Iowa. With the guidance of my professors at Buena Vista, I learned to do the same.

At first I thought I would teach youngsters like the third graders I had mentored during high school. A few days observing an elementary school classroom convinced me that high school students would be a better match for me. In my own life, I had come to know the truth of the statement that "we read to know we are not alone." I wanted to introduce young people on the cusp of adulthood to the books that would show them they weren't alone, as my teacher had done for me.

In the late 1990s, the internet was just beginning to be part of everyday life. My eyes were opened to its possibilities after a class assignment led me to the vast, dark computer lab on campus. Sitting at a keyboard, I typed the few details I had about my birth parents into the search engine, along with my own birth date, hoping that they were looking for me just as I was looking for them, and would recognize the clues. After many years of wondering who they were and what had led them to their fateful choice about my life, I now began my search in earnest.

I soon became a frequent participant in online adoption search forums. I had thought that the information contained in my now-missing adoption records was all I would ever know; I now discovered there was much more I could learn. Other adoptees shared their own experiences of trial and error, and from them I learned that I could petition the court to reveal all the non-identifying information it had about my birth mother and father. I hoped to find more specific information about them than I already had – maybe their first names, or birth dates, or where they had lived. I also learned I had a right to the medical records about my own birth. I eagerly communicated with the people on this forum and shared in their victories and disappointments. It felt like we were all on a treasure hunt for the peace that could only come from knowing the truth of who we were.

Mom and Dad knew I was searching; I had gone to them before I started, to ask their permission. I didn't want to hurt them; if they had told me not to look, I think I would have abided by their wishes, at least for a while. I told them how much I loved them and that no one could ever replace them. I'm sure my single-mindedness about my search made them uncomfortable at times, but they never expressed anything other than wholehearted support and encouragement. My brother Dustin was more mystified – he got why I was curious, but couldn't understand why I would want to find people who had tried to hurt me.

As I investigated my birth, I pursued my education with a businesslike attitude. I went to class, I studied, and I worked as many hours as I could at the flower shop. I socialized with my friends but avoided the college party scene. I took classes over the summer so I could graduate early. By the end of December 1999 I had earned my bachelor's degree and had my first teaching job, as a long-term substitute English teacher at a high school in Okoboji, Iowa, a small town about an hour from home. One of the things I left behind was my boyfriend; although some people thought we might end up married, I knew by then he was not the man for me.

My job was a temporary one; almost as soon as I arrived I had to start looking for a more permanent position at another school for the following year. My favorite class to teach was creative writing. It was an elective open only to seniors, and the students who took it did so because they had a sincere interest in writing. They worked hard and many had their own ambitions to study English. I learned that as much as I loved teaching, I loved the students even more. One young man in particular made a lasting impression. His story changed the direction of my career.

Isaac (not his real name) was a senior, with longish brown hair and thick glasses. He had a kind, gentle demeanor; although he was sometimes the target of teasing by his classmates, he took it in stride. He rarely spoke in class, but he stayed behind almost every day, striking up a conversation with me about whatever came into his mind, clearly needing someone to talk to. I was happy to listen, but what I learned drove me to my knees.

A year before I had arrived in Okoboji, Isaac had come home from school one day to find his mother and sister lying dead on the floor. This wasn't a random act of violence – the killer was his mom's estranged husband. No wonder Isaac didn't want to leave school after class – he no longer had a home of his own to go to!

I begged God for the wisdom to help him. I offered him a sympathetic ear, but I knew he needed the kind of professional help I was completely unqualified to give. Fortunately Isaac was surrounded by a strong community that gave him the love and support he needed; but nothing could ever make up for the loss of his mother and sister.

My eyes were suddenly opened to the issue of domestic violence. Before, it had seemed an abstract societal ill; now I knew it close-up as a tragic reality. I heard on the news that professional football player Rae Carruth, a wide receiver for the Carolina Panthers, was accused of hiring someone to kill his pregnant girlfriend because she refused to have an abortion. Tammy's pregnancy years earlier had shown me how a loving family's support can make it easier for a woman to choose life. In contrast, the Rae Carruth case showed how hard it must be for a woman whose pregnancy is met with violence from those close to her. I wondered again about my birth mother – had she been abused? My adoption records included information about my birth father's family, so I knew my mother had not been the victim of a stranger. But I had enough life experience by now to know that there might be more to the story than a simple teenage romance gone bad. Had my mother been pressured by someone to abort me? Part of me didn't want to dwell on such horrible thoughts. Yet I knew that we are all influenced by our beginnings, and I felt a growing determination to champion the cause of people hurt by domestic violence.

As the school year neared its end, I learned of a job opening at a domestic violence shelter in Spencer, Iowa. They were looking for someone to provide counseling and support to children who had been abused or had witnessed the abuse of others. Even though I didn't have a background in social work or psychology, I applied and was hired. Especially after my experience with Nathan, I felt like I was called to do this job. Instead of being in the classroom, I put my teaching skills to use by giving talks at area schools on dating violence and sexual abuse. I often met with troubled children at their schools, since their homes were unstable.

I loved the work but knew I was out of my depth. The women and children I met were in so much pain and in such desperate need of healing. I considered pursuing a PhD in psychology so I could work as a therapist with victims of domestic violence. I started taking undergraduate courses in psychology at Buena Vista University's Spencer campus with the intention of applying to a graduate program leading to a doctoral degree.

Every psychologist's first patient is herself, and I was no exception. The more deeply I got into psychology, the more I became aware that I was studying myself. The stress of my job, dealing with victims of horrific abuse at the hands of those who should have loved and protected them, triggered familiar feelings of fear and abandonment in me. But when those feelings came, I felt better able to understand them and put them in their proper perspective. I saw how my teen struggles with bulimia, alcohol, and sex had been feeble attempts at self-medicating my pain. Understanding its underlying cause made it easier to alleviate in a healthy way. Long walks, lots of exercise, and spending time outdoors became my therapy.

My search for my birth parents was moving at a glacial pace. In late 1999 I filed a petition to unseal my adoption records with the clerk of court in Palo Alto County. I received some non-identifying health information that revealed there were no significant health issues on either side of my birth family. I already knew that much from the adoption papers my parents had, but it was nice to see it confirmed in the official court documents. There were other avenues I could have pursued, but I was busy with my work and studies.

Through my job at the domestic violence shelter I had met two brothers, aged six and four, who stole my heart. They were cute and funny, typical boys with tons of energy, who had been exposed to far more adult dysfunction than any child should see. They sometimes imitated the bad examples they had seen by fighting and acting out. They often talked about the violence they witnessed at home; they were torn between their love for their father and their instinct to protect their mom from his anger. One weekend when I was on duty, I received a call on our crisis hotline from the boys' mother. She was hysterical; it was hard to figure out what she was saying between her sobs and her angry words. But at last I understood what she was saying, and could only answer her tears and anger with my own. Her two boys were dead; they had been killed in a suspicious accident involving their father. She had failed them. The system had failed them. I had failed them. We had not kept them safe.

I was at home in Storm Lake visiting my parents when the call came. I listened and gave her what counsel I could. What words could possibly console her? What help could I offer now that the worst had happened – now that her boys were gone? When we hung up, I collapsed to the floor of the upstairs bathroom in tears of impotent rage. Why is there so much evil in the world? How could a loving God permit two innocent children to die at the hands of the man who should have been their biggest defender? Then again, how could a mother end the life of her own child through abortion? Was it really that different? I couldn't make sense of any of it. I found some comfort in the thought that these boys I'd known and loved were in God's hands, out of harm's way – but why can't we make *this* world a better place for kids like them? Why should young children have to go through such hell?

# Five

*Before you can be anything, you have to be yourself.*
*That's the hardest thing to find.*
— E. L. Konigsburg

I WAS SHAKEN BY THE DEATHS of these two young boys. This tragedy could have – should have – been avoided. Those boys were dead because their families, their community, the "system" had let them down. I felt so ineffectual. I knew if I was ever going to be able to help people in situations like theirs, I would need more training and education. With that goal in mind, I continued to take courses toward a master's degree with an eye to one day earning a PhD in clinical psychology. I enrolled in a class taught by a brilliant senior faculty member who had the kind of background and experience I hoped to obtain someday. I respected him and sensed that he valued me as a student. I hoped he might advise me on my career plans and even recommend me to a PhD program.

Psychologists try to help their patients identify pivotal moments in their lives. These epiphanies, which often are linked to times of emotional distress, can lead to unexpected insights that prompt individuals to set new goals aligned with their true selves. To help his students better understand these critical junctures in a person's life, my professor assigned each of us to write a paper on a pivotal life experience of our own.

For me, there was only one pivotal experience to write about – that of being an abortion survivor. Everything that had happened to me since I had learned the truth about my birth flowed from that. I had tried to tell my story before, but now for the first time I systematically and unflinchingly put it on paper. It was the most difficult piece of writing I'd ever done, but I was determined. It took hours. I didn't spare myself anything. I wrote of the shocking moment of truth, my self-destructive struggles in its aftermath, the intense but futile search for my roots. It was the first time I'd shared this critical part of my life with anyone trained in psychology. I felt anxious yet hopeful – anxious about opening myself to scrutiny, hopeful about what I could learn from this trusted professional's opinion.

I did learn a great deal from my professor's response, but not what I expected. I earned an A for my technical analysis, but his comments in the margin were harsh.

One in particular has stuck with me all these years: "This must be a lie. Why would your parents tell you such an awful thing?"

I was floored. I'd been silenced again – this time not by my peers, but by a professional, someone esteemed in his field. I had made myself vulnerable, and I'd been struck down. But this time, I clearly recognized the reason for my professor's denial: he simply could not reconcile his support for abortion with the existence of a living, breathing survivor.

Ironically, writing a paper about a pivotal moment in my life led to another such moment. I had a vision of startling clarity that day about the choices before me. I could lie down and acquiesce in the silencing – or confront it. I chose to stand tall. I wanted to force people to face the contradiction that my existence posed to their ideology. But I knew that my word would not be enough – I needed verifiable documentation of how my life had begun.

⊰❧

A few months later I was accepted into a graduate program that could eventually lead to a PhD, but my aspirations had changed. In the fall of 2002, I enrolled in a program at the University of Iowa's Sioux City campus leading to a master's in social work. I continued to work in Spencer at my job, counseling victims of domestic abuse, but added a commute of about a hundred miles back and forth to Sioux City a couple of times a week for classes.

Over Thanksgiving break that year I went home to Storm Lake. My high school friend Kendra was back in town for her grandmother's funeral. Whenever she was around, she tried to pull together as many of our gang of friends from high school as she could. On Thanksgiving she organized a gathering at the local bowling alley. One of the people there was a mutual friend, Ryan, who had graduated a couple of years before we did. I had liked him from afar when we were in high school and began to admire him from a closer vantage point that evening – and discovered the feeling was mutual.

I slept at Kendra's house that night. I didn't have to tell her how attracted I was to Ryan – she could see that clearly! I wasn't sure, though, if or when or how I would ever see him again. Ryan lived in Sioux City and had returned to his apartment there after the get-together at the bowling alley. She boldly called him the following Saturday, inviting him to make the ninety-mile trip back to Storm Lake that night for another party! I went home to my parents' house after Kendra made her call, to get ready for the party. Dad was sitting at the kitchen table when I came in, and I caught him up on the news. "If Ryan comes back tonight, I think he will be the man I marry!" I added.

He came back.

How can I put into words what happens when two people fall in love? In the movie *Sleepless in Seattle* the character played by Tom Hanks describes: "Well, it was a million tiny, little things that, when you added them all up, they meant we were supposed to be together . . . and I knew it. I knew it the very first time I touched her. It was like coming home . . . only to no home I'd ever known. . . . I was just taking her hand to help her out of a car and I knew. It was like . . . magic." I think that just about captures what both Ryan and I felt.

Ryan later told me how surprised he was when Kendra called to invite him to come to Storm Lake a second time. He didn't think I'd have any interest in dating him! Little did he know I'd had a crush on him since high school. Our first real date was in Sioux City, after one of my classes. I got lost driving to his apartment, where we had planned to meet; he had to come find me. It's a bit of a cliché to say we talked all night, but we did. I told him my story, and my views on abortion, with some hesitation; I told him I would understand if he didn't want to make a second date. I was afraid he might not see things the way I did, afraid that he would be scared away. I quickly learned that nothing could frighten him away from me.

Ryan and I dated for two years before we got engaged. By then I had moved to Sioux City to be closer to him and to continue my work toward my master's degree. Ryan's quiet strength and unconditional love grounded me. I was happier than I had been since I was a young child. Every other guy I had dated treated the fact that I was an abortion survivor as an oddity and regarded my search for my birth family as a strange preoccupation. Ryan, though, embraced the truth about me simply because it made me the woman he loved. He encouraged my search for my birth family and always listened with a wise and willing heart.

I graduated with a degree in social work in May 2005 and got a job working as a supervisor for the Iowa Department of Human Services in Sioux City. For many years I had been an advocate for recovering addicts and victims of sexual abuse or domestic violence, working with them from the outside to get help and financial assistance from state-run programs. It was often a frustrating, unnecessarily bureaucratic process. I had seen firsthand how the system could fail; I knew good intentions and compassionate hearts weren't enough. Now I was working on the inside as part of a team that was committed to making the system more responsive to the people it served.

In October 2005, Ryan and I got married at the Methodist church in Storm Lake where I had been confirmed so many years before. Our families and friends joined us in a joyous celebration before we left for our honeymoon on South Padre Island off the Gulf Coast of Texas. We returned to Sioux City a week later and settled into a happy life as newlyweds.

A few weeks later I had an encounter that would turn out to be another pivotal moment in my life. From the time I found out about being an abortion survivor at the age of fourteen, I had been petrified of getting pregnant and somehow turning out "just like" my biological mother. I didn't want to take any chances that I would end up unmarried and pregnant at age nineteen, and although I could and should have made better choices about abstinence, I didn't. I got my first shot of Depo-Provera birth control at a Planned Parenthood facility in Storm Lake before I went to college. Later, when I was working in Spencer, I viewed the people who worked at the local Planned Parenthood clinic as colleagues in my work to prevent and treat domestic violence. I often visited that facility to post information in the hope that women would see it and contact us to get help dealing with domestic violence and sexual assault.

After moving to Sioux City, it took me a while to find a primary care physician with whom I felt comfortable. While I searched, I turned again to Planned Parenthood for birth control. At least I had some experience with them, I thought. So I made what would be a life-changing visit to the Planned Parenthood in Sioux City.

Driving my car up to the imposing building on Stone Avenue for the first time, I was struck by how much bigger it was than the little clinics I had visited in Storm Lake and Spencer. The high fence, the cameras, and the barbed wire around the building added to its daunting impression. Why would a Planned Parenthood clinic need such security? I chalked it up to being in the "big city." I kept my appointment and got my pills.

It wasn't long after that I began to hear whispers that this Planned Parenthood performed abortions. "Abortions? Planned Parenthood? That's impossible!" I told myself. It certainly raised a question in my mind, but not a big enough one to force me to investigate. As far as I was concerned, Planned Parenthood equaled birth control, and I was unaware of any downside to the use of contraceptives. Only much later did I learn of the detrimental effect they can have on a woman's body and on a marriage relationship. I continued to make regular visits to Planned Parenthood to fill my birth control prescription.

On a sunny but cool autumn day, I went to that Planned Parenthood clinic for the last time. As I was pulling out of the parking lot and onto the driveway, I looked out my driver's side window and saw a handful of men and women, young and old, standing outside the clinic holding signs and praying. I had never seen anything like this before in Sioux City, or anywhere else for that matter.

"You don't have to do this! We can help you!" an older man in a grey fedora called out as I started pulling my silver Pontiac Sunfire away. Confused, I rolled my window down. The look on his face reflected that he was both pleased and caught off-guard by my response. "You don't have to do this," he repeated, still some distance from my car, but close enough to converse.

"Do what? Get birth control? That's none of your business!" I blurted angrily.

Taken aback, he replied, "Oh! They do abortions here on Tuesdays. I thought that might be what you were here for," as he handed me a rosary and prayer card.

I was shaken to the core. So, it was true! I felt scared, shocked – and mortified: Me. A survivor. At an abortion clinic! As the man continued talking, I was flooded with emotion and knew I had to get away. I started rolling up my window. "Thank you," I managed to stammer as I tried to stuff the rosary into my glove box. "But I know about abortion. I'm an abortion survivor. My birth mother aborted me and I lived."

There. I had said it. Now this man knew what I had just discovered myself – an abortion survivor was patronizing an abortion clinic. I was so ashamed. After absorbing the initial shock of my statement, he grasped another rosary, and holding it high in the air, he shouted as I pulled away, "You should be here, not there!" pointing to the group of people praying on the sidewalk.

"You should be here, not there" pulsed through my pounding heart as I drove home. Beneath my wounded pride was a more deeply wounded heart. I felt stupid for not knowing Planned Parenthood did abortions. I felt guilty that I had been giving my money to an organization that performs them. And I felt challenged by the words of a man who gave his time to try to save lives like mine.

I *should* be there.

# Six

*For nothing is hidden that will not become evident, nor anything secret that will not be known and come to light.*
— Luke 8:17

Before I moved to Sioux City, my search for my birth family was done from a distance. Now I was living in the city of my birth, driving every day past St. Luke's Hospital, where I had survived the abortion.

I had written to St. Luke's in 1999 to request copies of my medical records. I asked for all "nursery, admission, discharge, and delivery room records" for a baby born on my birth date with the last name I was given in my adoption records, but the response I got was "we are unable to locate records on [you] being in our facility." I had called the hospital many times since, hoping that a different clerk might give a different answer. Unfortunately, the answer was always the same – no.

I fantasized about just walking into St. Luke's and asking for my records or visiting the maternity ward to find doctors or nurses who had been there in August 1977. But the truth is I was afraid to even walk into the building. My palms would sweat if I even glimpsed it while driving by on the highway.

I knew that being born in Sioux City didn't mean my birth family had lived there – St. Luke's is a regional center that draws patients from neighboring counties as well as the adjacent states of South Dakota and Nebraska. Still, it seemed a good place to pursue my search.

An idea I had picked up from one of the internet forums for adoptees was to put an ad in the local newspaper. I thought it over and decided to give it a try; but I agonized over the ad I wrote for the *Sioux City Journal*. My hands trembled as I pushed the "send" button on the e-mail. It cost sixty dollars to run the ad for one week. I didn't dare to hope that someone in my birth family would see the ad within that week, but I did think maybe a doctor or nurse who had been present at the time of the failed abortion might come forward with some information. No one ever responded.

Another suggestion I saw online was to hire a private investigator. I located one and placed a call to his office. I quickly dropped that idea when I learned his fee was five thousand dollars. "I don't have that kind of money," I said. "But if I did have it, what would you do to get the information?"

"It's easy," he replied. "My partner and I go into the courthouse and ask to see the adoption decree. When they pull the file, one of us distracts the guy while the other takes a photo of the info we need."

"No thanks," I said. "I'll come up with something else."

I already had the information about my birth family from the background report given to my parents before they adopted me – the one I had learned by heart as a child. It included the ages, aptitudes, and interests of my birth parents; their parents' occupations; and a last name. I wasn't sure the last name was really theirs – it's not an unusual name, and I thought it might be an alias assigned by the adoption agency. I suspected that the people who had been involved in obtaining the abortion might want to hide their identities.

But since it was all I had to go on, I used this name to try to discover who my parents were, using the resources of the Sioux City Public Library. I pored over the library's collection of yearbooks, hoping against hope to find someone with that last name who also was the right age to be my birth mother or father. No luck.

However, the background study had listed my birth mother's mother's occupation as a teacher in a nursing school. St. Luke's had a School of Nursing; could she have been affiliated with it? I went to the school's library to search its archives. I found that at the time I was born, there was a professor of nursing working there who was old enough to be my grandmother and whose last name was the one on my adoption records. I found myself getting excited, but I didn't dare let my hopes get too high.

Could this woman's husband have been a school superintendent, the job listed for him at the time I was born? I headed back to the library to search the history of Sioux City public schools. Bingo! I discovered a biographical blurb about a former school administrator with the same name who was married to a nurse! I felt a shiver run up my spine when I read he had earned a doctoral degree at the University of South Dakota – the school I had fallen in love with, then abruptly fled, so many years before.

I felt like Nancy Drew cracking the case. These *had* to be my birth mother's parents! But I couldn't find any proof that they even had children, much less a daughter who would have been nineteen in 1977. Despite the tantalizing clues, I felt I couldn't contact them until I found that missing link. If they had still lived in Sioux City, I might have been tempted to approach them, but I learned from public records that they had moved to another state. The harder I searched for my birth parents, it seemed, the more they eluded me.

Although I had been looking for my birth family for more than ten years, I had very little to show for my efforts beyond the information I had at the start. Everything I had tried led to a dead end. One morning after Ryan left for work, I went down to the basement to start the laundry before heading off to my office. My hands were sorting whites from darks, but my mind was racing over all the cul-de-sacs and dead ends I had encountered while trying to find out who I was, where I came from, and what had driven my birth mother to abort me. Finally, in a moment of profound discouragement, I fell to my knees on the cold concrete floor beside the washing machine and offered a prayer from the depths of my soul. "I can't do this anymore, Lord. If you want me to know the truth, you will have to show it to me. No matter what, thy will be done."

❧

In early 2007, my dad's father, Keith Cross, was admitted to a nursing home. At the age of eighty-four, he still had a clear mind, but his body was breaking down. He and I had always been close; my early interest in a career in government and law was inspired in part by him. He had served as mayor of his hometown of Mallard for many years and was always up for a no-holds-barred discussion about politics, or any other topic.

I made the two-hour drive from Sioux City to Emmetsburg to visit Grandpa many times that spring as he lay dying. During one of our last visits, he encouraged me to not abandon my search for my birth parents.

"I've given that up, Grandpa," I said. "If God wants me to know the truth, he'll show me."

"God helps those who help themselves," he replied. "Keep looking, Missy. You deserve to know the truth!"

With his words echoing in my ears, I called St. Luke's on my cell phone while I drove back home to Sioux City. I expected to hear, as I had before, that "there are no records pertaining to you in St. Luke's files." This time, though, the person on the other end of the line said something different. "I can't find anything in our records," she said. "Why don't you try the University of Iowa hospital? Your records from St. Luke's were probably transferred there when you were."

I had contacted that hospital before, as well, to no avail, but I tried again. The lady who answered the phone responded matter-of-factly: "If your records from St. Luke's are here, we'll send them to you. I'll send you a release form; once you return it to us, we will search our archives. If we find anything, we'll send it along."

All of a sudden it seemed so simple. Could this be the breakthrough I had been hoping – praying – for? It was. I filled out the release form on May 12, 2007. Less than two weeks later – on the day of my grandfather's funeral – the records I had been trying to find for a dozen years arrived in our mailbox.

The cover letter read: "In accordance with the signed authorization and in response to a recent request, please find enclosed copies of University of Iowa Hospitals and Clinics' medical record on the above named patient . . ."

I turned the page and read the notes made by the nurse. I weighed just 2 pounds, 14.5 ounces. Under "Complications of This Pregnancy" was written "Saline Infusion."

The Apgar test given to newborns to assess their health was administered; the score 6 (on a scale of 10) at one minute declined to just 2 at five minutes – a sign of critical distress. "Fetus active and weak cry," it read. "Transferred to ICU."

The following page was even more harrowing. "On August 24, saline infusion for an abortion was done but was unsuccessful." A saline abortion can only be done after sixteen weeks of pregnancy, when there is enough fluid in the amniotic sac surrounding the baby. A needle is inserted into the mother's uterus to withdraw as much amniotic fluid as possible; the fluid is replaced with a toxic saline solution. The baby, who has started to practice breathing in utero weeks earlier by inhaling amniotic fluid, now swallows the salt solution instead. It burns the baby's lungs and skin and eventually causes the heart to stop. In a "successful" saline infusion abortion, the mother goes through labor and delivers a dead baby. The abortion attempted on me was "unsuccessful" because I lived.

Most saline abortions are completed within forty-eight hours. But my records read, "On August 27th

Pitocin drip [to induce labor] was started." That's three days after the toxic salt solution was first injected. Did the abortionist wait to start the delivery process to be sure I was dead? I wondered if during that time he was checking for a fetal heartbeat. Did he detect how hard I was fighting for my life? I would have to fight even longer. Pitocin "was also repeated on August 28th. Her bag of water broke about 6:30 p.m. Pitocin drip was continued on the 29th." After five days of poison burning me from the outside in, I was "delivered spontaneously in bed by a nurse" at 3:40 p.m. on August 29th. "The baby is reported to have had a spontaneous weak cry," the report read, and was "brought to the Intensive Care Nursery" and treated for "respiratory distress syndrome."

The shock I felt as I studied the records overwhelmed me, and I sobbed for a long time. I cried for my newborn self, but also for my mother. What horror had she endured during those five days? Of course, I couldn't remember what had happened to me, but I felt sure she would never forget.

But as the tears subsided and I was able to look more closely at the pages in my hand, I felt a flurry of excitement: The full names of both my birth parents were printed at the top of the first page!

It felt like time had stopped. In a daze, I called Ryan at work. I was trembling all over as I tried to tell him what I had learned. I don't think I made any sense, but somehow he heard what I was trying to say: my long search for the names of my birth parents was over.

ST. LUKE'S MEDICAL CENTER                    SIOUX CITY, IOWA

GIVEN NAME OF BABY _____    SEX _____ HOSP. NO. 76444
DATE OF BIRTH 8/29/77 ___ TIME _____ COLOR _____  TYPE OF DELIVERY 150
DOCTOR _____ PEDIATRICAN _____  FEEDING Bottle
IDENTA BAND NO. 1034 ___ SIGNATURE OF NURSE APPLYING BAND, TAKING FOOT PRINTS
NAME OF MOTHER _____  PARA
NAME OF FATHER _____  PHONE
ADDRESS _____
RH A. pos. RELIGION _____ CIRCUMCISION _____ DISMISSAL DATE
ROOM NUMBER _____

---

**CONSULTATION**

Mother: ████████                              ████████, Baby Girl
Admit Intensive Care Nursery on August 29, 1977.     Dr. ██████
Date of Birth: 8/29/77·                               W-OBN
                                                      Dr. ██████

This baby was born prematurely to a 19-year-old unmarried mother.
According to the mother's hospital record, her last menstrual
period was 5/01/77, however, she reportedly stated she had had
no period in March or April. She was estimated to about 18 weeks
pregnant. On August 24th, Saline infusion for an abortion was
done but was unsuccessful. On August 27th, Pitocin drip was started.
It was also repeated on August 28th. Her bag of water broke about
6:30 PM. Pitocin drip was continued on the 29th. The baby was
delivered spontaneously in bed by a nurse. Apgar at one minute was

*A page from my medical record describes the abortion procedure.*
*I've blacked out the names to protect my birth parents' identities.*

My hands were still shaking as I sat down at the computer and googled the names printed on the page.

The online search for my birth mother's name revealed nothing. She had probably married, I thought; it would be hard to track her using her maiden name.

But within moments of typing my birth father's name, I had what I'd hoped for: a link to a web page that included his name. I had to absorb one more shock as I realized that the man I had spent most of my life searching for, the man who had given me life, lived in Sioux City, just a few miles away.

# Seven

*You can't always get what you want. But if you try*
*sometimes you might find you get what you need.*
—The Rolling Stones

For the next few days I followed the trail, trying to learn what I could about my birth father and his life in Sioux City. I went back to the library to look through the old yearbooks; now that I had his name it was easy to find his picture. My jaw dropped as I saw his face looking back at me. It was a masculine version of my own.

A search of the local phone book yielded his current address. A few clicks on the internet led me to where he worked in the IT industry. I jumped into my car and started driving. First, I drove slowly past his house. It was a tan split-level set back from the road on a cul-de-sac. The sight of a swing set on the lawn gave me a jolt. I had been so focused on finding out *who* my birth parents were that I hadn't really thought about the lives they were living. The swing set made it all very real. My birth father's life had gone on. He had a good job, a nice home, a wife and family. It had all seemed so easy when meeting him was just an abstract idea. Now I realized how high the stakes were. Whatever I decided to do next would affect not just one man, but a whole family.

Yes, now I had a name, and a place. But what did I really know? Nothing whatsoever about the nature of his relationship with my birth mother. Had she even told him she was pregnant with his child? Had he played any role in the abortion? Did he even know I survived?

Ryan and I talked late into the night about what to do next. Mom and Dad weighed in over the phone. After years of searching, suddenly I felt paralyzed. Weeks passed as I tried to decide what to do. In prayer, I felt an interior peace whenever I thought of sending my birth father a letter. So on Sunday, July 15, 2007, I took out my pen and began to write:

Dear Mr. [ . . . ],
I want to first of all apologize to you for any problems that receiving this letter at your work may possibly cause you. However, in weighing the options of sending correspondence to your home or work, I felt like this would be the option that would cause you the least trouble. I would guess that that very statement

may have you concerned at this point, so I guess that I should make my intent in this letter very clear, very fast.

There is no easy way to come out and say this, so here it is: I have reason to believe that you are my biological father. I recently received information in regard to my biological parents, and your name was given to me as my putative father. I was born August 29, 1977, at St. Luke's Hospital in Sioux City. My biological mother is [name].

I do apologize for dropping this bomb, so to speak, on you, and I am truly sorry if I am sending you this letter in error. If you are who I have been made to believe that you are, I would not doubt that you are very unsure of me and how I perceive my biological family. Besides, of course, being a bit curious and wanting to know more about where I came from, my other intention was to let you know that I am alive, well, happy, and healthy.

My entry into this world was far from perfect, and I know full well how incredibly blessed I am to even be alive, let alone perfectly healthy. I was adopted into a loving, happy family, and I have no ill will toward either of my biological parents or their families for the circumstances that surrounded my birth and adoption.

As you can see on the introduction to this letter, I, too, live here in Sioux City. It is fascinating to me that we may have crossed paths before, and I can't help but believe that I have ended up living in the Sioux City area for a reason.

I have done some research, and without sounding too intrusive, I must be honest. Comparing a childhood photo of me with a high school yearbook photo of you, there appears to be a resemblance between the two of us. Maybe this is merely a coincidence, but writing you this letter was a risk that I had to take.

For the sake of brevity, and considering that this letter may be reaching you inadvertently, I will keep this short. If you are who I have been made to believe that you are, please let this letter serve as my indication that I am first and foremost alive and well, grateful and not bitter, and interested in knowing more about you and the rest of the paternal side of my family.

All of this is new to me, so I am unsure of what the next step is. If you would like to write me back, either by e-mail or mail, that would be a starting point. I can understand that I may be a part of your life that you wish to leave in the past, and if that is the case, I can respect that, and I will respect you in your decision not to respond to this letter or have any contact with me. Again, this is the risk that I am taking by contacting you, but I believe that doing this is the right thing to do for me and for you (letting you know that I am happy and healthy).

Again, if this letter is reaching you mistakenly, and you have no reason to believe that you are my biological father, I do apologize for taking up your time with this matter. If you are who I have been made to believe that you are, I apologize for any strife that this correspondence lends itself to. Of course, one way or the other, I look forward to hearing from you.

Sincerely,

Melissa Ohden

Rather than entrust my letter to the corner mailbox, I took it to the main post office downtown and personally handed it to the postal clerk. The envelope seemed so light! It should have been heavier – it contained so much of myself.

I tried to accept the possibility that I might not get a response. But the truth is, I was sure my birth father would answer right away. I had included my home address and my e-mail in the letter. Now every time there was a knock on the door, I felt a surge of anticipation – followed by disappointment. I think I wore out the "refresh" button on my computer checking for a response. Ryan was working the night shift, so he was home while I was at work. I called him every day around the time I knew the mail would be delivered. He hated feeling like he was letting me down when he had to repeat that nothing had arrived. He finally told me to stop asking. His words were a reminder that we were in this together; I didn't suffer my suspense alone.

As the weeks passed with no response, my mind examined all the possible reasons. Have I made a horrible mistake? Does my birth father think I am lying? Maybe he never even knew about me! The hardest question of all was, what would I do if he never answered?

While I waited, I continued to research my birth mother and her family. I hit a wall because I didn't have her married name. But I was now 100 percent sure that the last name on my adoption record was hers. I reasoned that if I could connect her to the couple with that last name whom I had discovered previously, I could track her down through them. I knew the husband had earned a doctoral degree at the University of South Dakota; so I made the forty-five-minute drive to Vermillion for the first time since I'd left it in the snowstorm at the end my first difficult semester, to look for his dissertation in the college library. I found it easily and saw on the first page the proof I had been seeking: the volume was dedicated to his four children, one of them my birth mother.

Google – by now my best friend – yielded an out-of-state address for the couple I was now sure were my birth mother's parents.

On August 27, 2007, I wrote them a letter similar to the one I had written to my birth father. I assured them I had no ill will toward them or their daughter. I implored them to pass along my letter to her. As I had to my birth father, I wrote that I would understand if they decided not to respond. Again, I didn't really mean it. Accept, maybe – but understand?

Fortunately, I didn't have to do either. Two days after I mailed the letter to my mother's parents, their response appeared in my mailbox. Ironically it arrived on my thirtieth birthday.

Ryan had been working away from home that day, so I was the one who checked the mailbox when I got home from the office. I stared at the hand-addressed envelope for several long minutes before tearing open the flap. Two photographs fluttered out as I unfolded the single piece of typewritten stationery. It was signed by my grandfather. With a knot of excitement in my stomach, I began to read:

> Dear Melissa,
>
> It was a surprise to discover your letter in our mailbox today but we have known for thirty years that such a letter might one day arrive. Our daughter [ . . . ] did indeed deliver a baby girl on August 29, 1977, at St. Luke's Hospital in Sioux City. Your letter indicates that you are aware that a live birth was not the intended outcome when she was first hospitalized. We are relieved to know that you suffer no lasting effects of your obviously premature birth.

The letter went on to give details of their daughter's life – her birth, education, and marriage. It continued:

We have been estranged from [our daughter] since the fall of 2002. We do know how to contact her and her twin sister does occasionally see her. To the best of our knowledge, [she] never revealed your existence to her husband or their two daughters. Because of that, we cannot say whether or not she would be willing to acknowledge you at this point in time.

After providing some family health background, he concluded:

We have included two photos of [our daughter] for you. The one on the left is her high school gradua-tion photo, taken in 1975. The one on the right is from 2003. We are pleased to know that your childhood years were happy and that you have done so well in school and in your career. We hope we have been able to fill in some of the blanks for you.

I read it a dozen times. My emotions shifted with each reading. I was thrilled that I had received any response at all. I was grimly amused by the letter's euphemistic ref-erence to the failed abortion as a "premature birth," as if it were just one of those things that happen in pregnancy, rather than the result of a deliberate act. I was puzzled by the claim that my birth mother and her parents were estranged. Were they really so alienated that my grand-parents couldn't forward to her a letter as significant as mine? And if so, what had caused a rift so deep? I had a sense of foreboding; something was not quite as it seemed.

I turned to the photographs and looked intently for the first time at the face of the woman in whose womb I had lived, and nearly died. I had imagined this moment a thousand times since I had learned I was adopted when I was a little girl. I desperately wanted to see myself in her – to see a physical manifestation that would prove our intimate relationship. In both photos she smiled sweetly, although I thought I could detect a twinge of sadness behind her smile in the more recent picture. She was a lovely woman, with light-brown hair, brown eyes, and fair skin. I could see a similarity in the shape of our eyes, but she didn't have my blue-black hair, green eyes, or olive complexion. I was not her. She was not me.

The poet T. S. Eliot once wrote that "the end of all our exploring will be to arrive where we started and know the place for the first time." For years I had been trying to go back to the beginning to discover my true identity. Reading that letter and looking at the pictures helped me realize I had been looking in the wrong place. My true identity didn't come from my birth parents, but from my Creator. I was a child of God and that meant I was never – not even for a second – unwanted. The letter I had received wasn't what I had hoped for, and yet it set me free.

# Eight

*We must be willing to let go of the life we have planned,
so as to have the life that is waiting for us.*
—Joseph Campbell

My long search for my birth parents had brought me tantalizingly close to them, and yet they were still out of reach. My birth father had not responded to my letter, and my birth mother's parents had refused to help me contact her. I wasn't at a dead end, but the path forward was unclear. I knew *about* them, but I didn't know *them*, as individuals, and I wasn't sure I ever would. I was disappointed but was given the grace to "leave the past to God's mercy, the present to God's love, and the future to God's providence," as the old saying goes. His providence was abundant indeed, for I had learned, just days before receiving the letter from my birth mother's parents, that I was pregnant with our first child.

Ryan and I had been hoping to start a family. When I thought I might be expecting, I took seven at-home pregnancy tests just to be sure! I whispered the news to Ryan one morning while he was still lying in bed, saying, "I think maybe you're going to be a daddy!" We were both overjoyed.

As a first-time mother, I was hyperaware of the changes taking place in my body. Every nauseous morning, every strange craving, and every fluttery kick was a vivid reminder of the new life growing within. My excitement was tempered by an unexpected sadness. My birth mother must have experienced some of the same sensations! How could she have felt what I was feeling, and still chosen to end my life? The thought stirred up fears I thought I had left behind. I was plagued by a dread that somehow I wouldn't be able to carry our baby to term, or would die in childbirth. There was absolutely no medical basis for my worry; I was healthy and fit and had no reason to expect complications. But I had cheated death once before; maybe now death would demand its due.

I knew such thoughts were irrational and superstitious, but I couldn't shake them. My ob/gyn did his best to reassure me. An ultrasound at twenty weeks allayed some of my anxiety, but it wasn't without its surprises. I had been sure our baby was a boy since the moment I found out I was pregnant. So much for a mother's intuition . . .

Ryan, who I think had secretly wanted a girl all along, was thrilled. I was too. But the tears began to flow as I realized that everything in my background had led to this precious new life. How could I regret even a moment of my past, if it had led to this? We named our unborn baby Olivia; no child of mine would be nameless!

In the movie *It's a Wonderful Life,* a suicidal George Bailey is given a glimpse by his guardian angel of what life would have been like for the people he loves had he not been born. "You've been given a great gift, George," says Clarence Odbody, his angel. "A chance to see what the world would be like without you." The ultrasound image of our baby gave me the great gift of seeing the face of the child who would be born because I had lived. I felt a fearsome responsibility to my daughter to use what had happened to me to make her world a place where all babies are cherished.

A few months before my ultrasound, I had spoken out for the first time on the issue of abortion. Ever since my encounter with the man outside Planned Parenthood, I had known I needed to, as he said, "be here, not there," and take a stand for the sanctity of all human life. I had struggled, though, to find the right time and place. I wanted to speak out in a way that was true to both my feminist philosophy and my pro-life convictions.

Even though popular culture and elite opinion regarded the phrase "pro-life feminist" as an oxymoron, I believed the pro-life position was profoundly pro-woman, too. Like Alice Paul, the author of the first Equal Rights Amendment, I saw abortion as "the ultimate exploitation of women." When I discovered Feminists for Life (FFL), I knew I had found a pro-life organization I could whole-heartedly support. I was immediately drawn to its mission statement: "Women deserve better than abortion."

Toward the end of 2006, I wrote to FFL, telling them my own story and expressing my thanks for their work. I didn't expect any response but was happy to be added to their mailing list. A message went out to that list in the summer of 2007, asking for volunteers who would be willing to share a pro-life feminist message on college campuses that fall. I had been waiting for the right opportunity to tell my unique story; was this it? Ryan and I talked through the implications of going public. He was supportive but practical and protective too. Better than I, he foresaw the far-reaching consequences that sharing my story would have for our life. I felt so aligned with FFL's mission, though, that any reservations I had were quickly swept away.

Soon after I volunteered, I got a call from Valerie Schmalz, one of FFL's executives. I felt like I had been through the third degree by the time we were done. She questioned every detail of my life story. She checked my references, contacted my family, and reviewed the medical records I had received just a few months earlier. My story checked out, and in August I got on a plane to Washington, DC, where I was briefed on the issues and given media training on how to communicate in an effective, non-polarizing way. It was a surreal experience to be trained on how best to talk about myself!

My first speech was the next day at a Capitol Hill briefing. The training had prepared me mentally, but emotionally I was a basket case. I was away from Ryan for the first time since our wedding. The hormones surging through my body were playing havoc with my emotions, too, but at that point I didn't know that pregnancy was to blame!

Among the people in the audience that day were women who had had abortions they later regretted. Meeting them moved me deeply. In each of their eyes I saw the possibility that my own birth mother had the same regrets. My greatest fear was that I might say something that could cause these women, and by extension my own mother, pain. I needn't have worried. Their heartfelt response confirmed that speaking out was the right thing – for them as well as for myself.

I spoke at several events over the next few months and did media interviews. At one event on a college campus in North Carolina, I revealed that I was pregnant. The prayers and good wishes that flowed from the people who heard my story lifted me up whenever my irrational fears threatened to overtake me. In January 2008, around the time of the anniversary of *Roe v. Wade*, I returned to Washington, DC, to speak to college students in town for the annual March for Life. I shared with them the news that we were expecting a girl. I'll never forget the sound of their cheers when I said, "I'm pretty sure she is going to be pro-life!"

By early 2008, I was preparing for Olivia's birth, speaking out against the violence of abortion, working full time, and being a wife to Ryan. There was no time to worry about the disappointments of my search for my birth family. The letter from my birth mother's parents cut off the only clear avenue I had to reach her. And although my birth father and I lived in the same city, his deafening silence in response to my letter left little doubt that he wanted no contact.

Still, every once in a while I would google their names, hoping something would come up that would provide some insight into their lives and decisions. New records were being made available on the internet each day; surely, I thought, I will eventually find what I am looking for. My main thought was that I would find something that would give me my birth mother's married name and location.

One cold winter's night in March 2008 I was lying in bed watching TV, seven months pregnant and feeling too heavy and uncomfortable to do much of anything. I had my laptop beside me, and I idly typed my birth father's name into the search engine during a commercial break.

It had been a few months since I had searched his name, but I didn't expect to find anything new. I wasn't prepared for the headline that popped up as the first result of my search. It came from an issue of the *Sioux City Journal* that had been published two months earlier. It was my father's obituary.

The room spun around me as I tried to absorb this news. I learned he had died suddenly, at the age of fifty-one. Waves of self-doubt broke over me. Why hadn't I tried harder to meet him? Now it was too late!

That night as I lay sobbing in Ryan's arms, I vented my rage and grief to God. "After years of searching, I found him – and now I've lost him! How can this be your plan?" It seemed like a cruel trick of fate rather than the design of a loving Father.

But as my tears subsided, I remembered that God's ways are not our ways. Deep in my heart I knew I was being called to accept what I could not change, and to be patient. I had been comforted by a verse from Jeremiah so many years before at my confirmation; now I clung to another verse from the prophet: "For I know the plans I have for you, declares the Lord, plans to prosper you and not to harm you, plans to give you hope and a future." I would just have to wait.

🔊

The most immediate plan for the future was Olivia's birth. The decision about where to have our baby should have been easy. There were several hospitals in Sioux City, but St. Luke's stood out as the best for neonatal care. Ironically, I was living proof of its expertise in saving the lives of fragile newborns. But its image was so deeply tied to my intended death that I didn't think I could walk through its doors, much less give birth there. As my due date crept closer, my doctor gently nudged me toward a decision. He knew the reason for my fears but said, "If anything goes wrong, Melissa, it's the best place for you and the baby." I knew I had to do what was best for Olivia. With Ryan's encouragement, I signed us up for a birthing class at St. Luke's.

Still, as St. Luke's automatic doors slid open on a bitterly cold Saturday morning, I was filled with dread. Ryan and I nervously entered a small square waiting room near the front entrance. There were about ten other couples in the room, most of them first-timers like us. Little did they know how hard I was working to keep myself together. Ryan did his best to comfort me and calm me down.

The class was supposed to begin at ten o'clock, but the hour came and went. Eventually a nurse poked her head in to tell us that our teacher had had car trouble but was on her way. As the clock struck eleven and inched toward noon, I had to fight a mighty urge to flee. I had been praying for wisdom, asking God if giving birth at St. Luke's was the right thing to do; maybe this delay was a sign that it was not!

Luckily the teacher arrived before I could make a run for it. She led us into the auditorium to begin our class. Lori introduced herself and apologized for the delay. Car problems weren't the reason for the late start, she admitted. The hospital had forgotten to schedule someone to teach our class, so they had hurriedly gone down the staff roster until they found a nurse willing to come in on such short notice. Everyone in the room groaned, but her next words left me speechless. "Don't worry," she said. "I'll make it up to you, I promise. I've worked here since the mid-1970s, and I have a lot of wisdom that I can impart to you."

The significance of her words sank in. Lori had been a maternity nurse at St. Luke's when I was born – she had to know who I was! "Missy, don't . . . not now!" Ryan whispered urgently. He understood that all the breathing and relaxation tips were passing me by, that I could focus only on when and how to approach this woman. "I won't!" I breathed back. "Not yet!"

When the class broke for lunch, Lori headed for the ladies' room. I followed her there and waited until she was ready to leave. I felt a surge of courage as I introduced myself and said, "I think you might know who I am. I survived a saline abortion here in August of 1977." I spoke softly, not wanting to be overheard and afraid of how she might respond. Other women came and went, oblivious of our conversation. Lori's shock turned to tears as she looked into my eyes and said, "Of course I know who you are! You look just like your grandmother."

I had seen photos of my biological grandmother; although I couldn't see any resemblance, it was clear that Lori had glimpsed something in me that reminded her of the nurse she knew. We spoke intimately for a few moments more, as I told her how my life had unfolded after I had left St. Luke's as a helpless infant and about our plans for Olivia's birth. Lori said, "We never wanted you to find out. The doctors and nurses, we just never wanted you to find out."

I learned later that my survival had taken place in the context of an effort in the local community, led by a consortium of churches and joined by pro-life doctors and nurses, to persuade St. Luke's to end its participation in abortion – a struggle that eventually succeeded. I knew nothing of that larger debate at the time. I was touched by Lori's kind words and welcomed her frank confirmation of what had happened to me. But I couldn't share her wish that I had never learned the truth. "Thank you for caring so much about me," I said as we left the restroom, "but I wouldn't have it any other way."

# Nine

*Nearly all the best things that came to me in life have*
*been unexpected, unplanned by me.*
— Carl Sandburg

LORI WASN'T ON DUTY at St. Luke's when Olivia
was born one early April morning, but the young delivery
nurse who was knew my story. "Lori told us all about
you," she reassured me with a smile.

My contractions had started two days earlier while
I was still at work. That night, Ryan and I nervously
headed to the hospital only to be sent home to wait a
little longer. The next day I was admitted to the hospital
at noon. When after fourteen hours of strenuous labor
Olivia hadn't made her appearance, the doctors and
nurses began to prep me for a C-section. I dreaded the
idea, but was so exhausted I told Ryan I was ready to give
up. He looked at me with steely determination and said,

"Oh no, you're not!" I felt a surge of strength and at last Olivia was born, at two o'clock in the morning. At the very place where I had been most vulnerable, I now felt powerful and whole.

Olivia was a healthy baby overall, but like many newborns (including me) she developed jaundice. Just one day after bringing her home, we were back at St. Luke's for treatment. I stayed in the hospital with her. I marveled at how my fussing daughter would immediately calm down in my arms. "Nothing surprising about that," the neonatal nurse said. "She knows you!"

"She knows you." Of course she does! The intimate bond between mother and child begins long before birth. Newborns immediately recognize the voice of their mother. At one time I would have been angry that the newborn me had been cruelly deprived of the comfort of my birth mother's voice and arms. Now, though, with my own daughter nestled securely against my breast, I felt a surge of compassion for the woman who had carried me, and for what she had lost.

Olivia came home from St. Luke's for the second time two days later, and we soon settled into a happy routine. I was fortunate to have three months of maternity leave, and even more lucky to have the help of my mother-in-law, who stayed with us for a few days to help out.

A few weeks after Olivia's birth, on a bright May morning, I stepped outside to collect the mail. Among the bills and catalogs was a handwritten envelope with a return address I didn't recognize. Thinking it must be a card from someone congratulating us on Olivia's birth, I casually opened it as I walked inside – but stopped short as I began to read.

It had been four months since my birth father had died, and nearly a year since my letter to him. I had given up hoping that I would ever hear anything from his family. Yet here in my hands was a letter from his aunt, Vicki, acknowledging and accepting me as his daughter. She did not know I had already discovered that my father had died and gently broke the news. "I am so sorry that this happened to you," she wrote.

I was stunned. I called Ryan at work to tell him the news, then went to the computer to send an e-mail to Vicki at the address she had provided. As we tried to arrange a date to meet, I discovered that she had contacted me a month earlier, via a website I had set up in support of my pro-life speeches. I had been so absorbed in Olivia's birth that I had overlooked it.

It took several weeks for us to find a date that worked for both of us – another lesson in patience! I was a nervous wreck when I pulled up to the Perkins restaurant where Vicki and I had agreed to meet. I was running late, with Olivia in tow, and was afraid Vicki would think I had decided not to keep our date. It felt like all eyes were on me as I struggled to get Olivia out of her car seat. As I entered with my baby in my arms, an older woman with kind eyes and a warm smile came up beside me. "Let me help you," she said. "I knew it was you, Melissa, because you look just like him." Our tears were the words our hearts couldn't express.

My apprehension melted away as we settled into a booth and began to talk. The two hours we spent together that day flew by as we filled in the pieces of the past thirty years.

Vicki told me that my father's death had been a shock from which his family was still reeling. My letter had been discovered in his top desk drawer after his funeral. His boss gave it to his wife a few days later, when she came to the office to meet with the human resources staff to sort through some financial matters. The letter had been opened; she read it right away and its contents left her stunned. Her grief over his death was now compounded by the realization that he had kept my existence from her. I can't imagine how devastating it must have been to learn that the man she loved and lived with for so many years had kept something so important from her. My heart surged with compassion for her; her questions for her husband were even more urgent than my own, yet neither of us could ask them.

What had he thought when he received it? And what had kept him from responding? Had he worried about finding the right time and words to tell his wife, never expecting to die so soon? "I am sure he didn't know about you until he got the letter," Vicky suggested. "I think the reason he hadn't thrown it in the shredder was that he wanted to contact you, but didn't know how to tell his wife. If he had no intention of contacting you, he would have tossed the letter." I wanted to believe she was right, but would never know for sure.

Vicki had learned the news from her brother, who had been with my father's widow at the time she learned the news. He was a financial advisor and was helping her take care of things. Both he and Vicki were trying to help their sister – my grandmother – and her family cope with the loss of a beloved son, husband, and father. But Vicki's heart also broke for me as she realized that I, too, had suffered a loss. She googled my name and found my website, but, upon reading that I was pregnant, decided to wait until after our baby was born to contact me.

Vicki sat in stunned silence as I told her what I had learned from my medical records about my survival. She knew the bare facts from my letter to my father and from my website, but she wept as I filled in the details.

She filled in some blanks for me, too. She told me my father was one of three brothers who had grown up in Sioux City. I knew from my adoption records that his mom was a teacher and his dad was a farmer. But from Vicki I got a sense not just of what they did, but the kind of people they were. I was glad to learn that my father had been raised by loving parents in a happy home.

Vicki also knew my birth mother. She told me my birth parents both had aspired to careers in teaching. They dated for four years; everyone had expected they would marry. It comforted me in one way to know I had been conceived in love; but it made abortion even harder to understand.

What had driven my birth parents apart? Vicki told me my birth mother's family had been unhappy about their relationship, but she didn't pinpoint a reason. None was really needed; teenage romances – even ones as long-standing as theirs – break up all the time. Vicki told me my birth father's family never knew their son's girlfriend was pregnant. The question that hung in the air was obvious: Had he?

As we talked, I began to get a sense of the father I would never meet. Vicki gave me a photograph of him and emphasized his community spirit, his sense of humor, and his commitment to his family. An early first marriage had ended in divorce. He had become a Catholic when he married for a second time. Although the first child of that marriage had died at birth, both he and his wife were devoted to their second child, a daughter, who was now a teenager deeply affected by the loss of her dad.

Vicki and I forged a close friendship that day – we just clicked. It felt like we had known each other forever. I was so grateful for the information she shared with me, but one thing was hard to accept. She told me that although my father's brother and some members of the extended family knew about my existence, they had decided not to tell his parents about me right away. The shock of his death was still too raw, and the feelings of his wife and daughter too fragile. Vicki didn't know when, or if, my grandparents would learn the truth. That was hard news to hear and accept.

A few weeks later I was upstairs at home when the doorbell rang. It was early morning and I was still in my pajamas after a busy night with Olivia. I wasn't expecting company and was sure the visitor was a door-to-door salesman. I was relieved when the ringing stopped – Olivia had just fallen asleep and I wanted her to stay that way!

Later that day I went out to the mailbox on the curb. As I walked back toward the house, I noticed an envelope wedged in the front door. I grabbed it and stuck it in the pile of mail. Indoors, I examined it more carefully and found it was a message to me written in a shaky, unfamiliar hand. My heart began to pound as I read:

May 31, 2008

To Melissa:
On May 23rd my wife + I received the shock of our life. We have a granddaughter + great granddaughter that we did not know we had. We have your picture and 2 website pages. I will keep this short. I would be delighted to meet you as I have so many things I could tell you. I hope and pray that you will make contact.

The letter was signed "from your bio-Grandfather Don." My grandfather had been the one ringing my doorbell a few hours earlier – and I had ignored him!

May 31 - 08

To Mellin:
On May 23rd my wife + I
received the shock of our life. We have
a granddaughter + that Granddaughter that we
did not know we had.
we have your picture and
3 website pages. I will keep this short.
I would be delighted to meet you as
I have so many things I could tell you.
I hope and pray that you will make
Contact.

From your bio-grandfather
Don ██████████

*My paternal grandfather left this note at my front door.*

I called Ryan right away, but I waited a week to dial
the number my grandfather had provided along with his
note. I felt unprepared to meet him. I was just getting
used to being a new mother; I didn't know if I was ready
to be a new granddaughter as well. The weight of my
grandfather's expectations, and my own, pressed down
on me.

Finally I got over my own insecurities and started to
think more about the feelings of the man who had lost
his son and then "received the shock of [his] life." I knew
too well how hard it is to wait. At last I placed the call.

My stomach was in knots as the phone rang. A woman's
voice answered. My grandmother! I asked if Don was at
home. "Who's calling?" she asked.

"It's Melissa Ohden," I replied.

"He has been expecting your call," she said, as she passed the receiver to her husband. In that short exchange I sensed a chilly, even fearful resignation.

In contrast, my grandfather's voice was overflowing with excitement. We quickly made plans to meet at the Crystal Café, his favorite place to eat in South Sioux City.

I think I spent more time getting dressed for our meeting the next day than I did for my wedding! I was still carrying extra pounds from my pregnancy. I'd been living for the past month in Ryan's old shirts and my gym pants with their forgiving elastic waists. Now I had to find something in my closet that fit. I really wanted to look my best to make a good impression.

I needn't have worried. The minute I drove with Olivia into the parking lot at the café, my grandfather rushed out the door to greet us. He embraced me, and as we lived this private moment in a public space, he offered Olivia and me his unconditional acceptance.

We talked for hours that day, and the tears flowed for both of us. Grandpa couldn't get over the resemblance between me and the son he missed so much. We both were overwhelmed by God's goodness in bringing us together. Something he never knew he had lost had miraculously been found. But he had as many questions for his son as I did. His son had never confided in him that his girlfriend was pregnant; had his son even known? If he had, why hadn't he turned to his parents for help? They would have raised their grandchild without a moment's hesitation. We helped each other accept that we would never learn the answers in this life.

Grandpa, Olivia, and I began meeting every week or so. Ryan met him when he stopped by the house in his pickup truck, but more often Olivia and I would meet him at the Crystal Café. He was a fixture there, and as his friends and acquaintances passed our booth, he would introduce me as his granddaughter and show off Olivia, his first great-granddaughter, to the other customers. He even made sure the cooks and waitresses knew who we were! This was a new sensation, and I felt uncomfortable at first. I had never shared the names of my birth family with anyone other than Ryan and my own family. Now all of a sudden my identity was out in the open.

My discomfort didn't last long. It gave way to gratitude for this generous, loving man who was willing to embrace me with an open heart and mind. Finding out about me helped him make sense of things that had happened in the past. Grandpa Don told me that his son and my birth mother had "gone steady" for four years. He got to know her well, and liked her. He was happy with the idea that they might marry one day. They continued to date after they went to college – he to Augustana University in Sioux Falls, South Dakota, she to the University of South Dakota in Vermillion. But their relationship ended abruptly during that first year apart.

"I thought they broke up because of the accident," he recalled with regret. "After her father showed up on our doorstep and demanded that our son 'never darken his door' again."

Accident? What accident? My mind raced. I didn't press Grandpa Don for details that day. But what I later learned helped a few more pieces of the mystery of my existence fall into place.

The "accident" referred to a car accident that occurred in the fall of 1975. As I heard it from his family, one day when my father was a senior in high school, he was part of a crowd of teenagers gathered in the school parking lot after a sporting event to talk and horse around. My father sat in the driver's seat of his car, and playfully revved the engine. He did this several times as his friends gathered around the car, laughing. Suddenly the car slipped into gear and lurched forward, pinning a girl and her boyfriend against the wall of the school. In horror, my father jumped out of the car while his friends ran for help.

The ambulance came and whisked the injured students away, while the police took statements from my father and the witnesses who gathered around. The investigation concluded that it had been an accident – that my father had not touched the gear shift and that his revving of the engine was not the cause of the car's malfunction. My father felt great remorse about what had happened, but he was not legally at fault.

The girl who had been pinned was seriously injured, and the finding of "no fault" was no comfort to her or to her family. Her parents seethed with anger, which was heightened by the fact that they knew my father well. He had dated their other daughter – my mother – for four years. The girl who was injured was my mother's twin sister, and in the accident's aftermath her parents did everything they could to break up my mother and father.

It was hard for me to take all this in. It sounded like the plot of a soap opera – fiction rather than fact. But it was very real. My birth parents continued their relationship despite the strong opposition from her parents. The animosity toward my birth father endured, and played a decisive role in what happened nearly two years later, when my mother discovered she was pregnant with me. A senseless accident for which no one was to blame had altered the course of many lives, including mine.

# Ten

*Real life seems to have no plots.*
— Ivy Compton-Burnett

MY TIME AT HOME with Olivia was busy and blissful. I loved being a mom! Ryan was a natural father, and seeing him tenderly care for our daughter deepened my love and appreciation for him. We were no longer just a couple; we were a family. Olivia brought great joy into our lives.

I dreaded going back to work at the Department of Human Services when my maternity leave ended. It wasn't that I didn't like my job – I did! I had a great group of colleagues and I found the work fulfilling. I knew the work we did for families in crisis was important. Yet whenever I thought about leaving my tiny baby in someone else's care, I would fall apart. I came across this quote from Arianna Huffington, founder of the Huffington Post: "I think while all mothers deal with feelings of guilt, working mothers are plagued by guilt on steroids." She is right!

But guilt or no guilt, I had to work. We definitely needed both Ryan's income and mine to keep our family afloat, and our excellent health insurance came through my employment with the state of Iowa. With heavy hearts we found a safe, nurturing daycare for Olivia. It was located between Ryan's office and our home, and the experienced, loving staff put me at ease. We soon settled into a new routine.

In late 2008, I received an invitation to speak the following January at Siouxland Right to Life's annual event commemorating the thirty-sixth anniversary of *Roe v. Wade.* I accepted with some trepidation. I had grown comfortable telling my story to anonymous audiences far away. Now I would be speaking to my neighbors and friends; I feared I would be like the prophet "honored everywhere except in his own hometown." Mom and Dad and Ryan's parents came to hear me speak; I wondered if any of my birth family would be in the room as well.

The following day the *Sioux City Journal* ran a front-page story, complete with a picture, reporting on my speech.

SIOUX CITY – About 500 people Sunday heard a series of speakers, including one who survived an abortion procedure, say it is time anti-abortion Siouxlanders took firmer actions to change the societal tide of acceptance for abortion.

Held to coincide with the January 1973 *Roe v. Wade* Supreme Court decision affirming a woman's right to seek an abortion, speakers at the Siouxland Pro-Life Interfaith Prayer Memorial at Central Baptist Church said more than 50 million people have been lost through the choice of abortion. A series of people, from age 1 to 36, came to the front of the church carrying a rose to give representation to the 36 years of legalized abortion.

Melissa Ohden of Sioux City went public with her journey through what she called shame, guilt, embarrassment and anger of having been aborted yet surviving at about 23 weeks of gestation while weighing two pounds. [I later confirmed that the abortion took place at 31 weeks of gestation.]

Ohden was adopted by Sioux City parents, and said she wished her birth mother, who was in college, had given greater thought to options of adoption or becoming a single parent.

"I was wanted," she said.

Ohden frequently cried as she worked through her story and expressed gratitude that her parents made the choice to raise a baby predicted to have many health problems after living through a saline abortion procedure at a Sioux City hospital in 1977.

"I stand before you today with no ill effects from the abortion attempt," she said.

Ohden earned two college degrees, works for the Department of Human Services, volunteers for Feminists For Life, is married and in April 2008 had a daughter, Olivia, at the hospital where the procedure to abort her 31 years prior occurred.

At the end of her 25-minute speech, she challenged the crowd. "I challenge all of you to refuse to choose between women and children – it doesn't have to be either-or," Ohden said.

Gregg and Mary Gesche of Merrill, Iowa, have attended several of the Siouxland Pro-Life Interfaith prayer services and said Ohden's speech ranked among the best.

"How can a person not be affected by her testimony? She's a messenger to the people, to instill change in them, to spur us on to keeping fighting against this evil of abortion," Gregg Gesche said.

Wow. I wasn't expecting that! What had I done? I knew from my experience with Lori at St. Luke's that there were people in town who knew what had happened and who my birth parents were. Now I feared I had exposed them to scrutiny they didn't expect or deserve. In my speech I'd made clear that I had forgiven everyone involved, especially my birth mother. I was heartsick with worry that this message of forgiveness had not come through the filter of the media.

Overnight, my anonymity disappeared. I was recognized one day when I stopped at a salon to get my nails done. A woman who worked at Olivia's daycare center pulled me aside to tell me she had done some research after reading the *Journal* story and had made an educated guess about my background. "I read more about your story, Melissa," she said. "I think I know who your birth father is. I cared for his other daughter when she was a little girl." She was amazed by the coincidence; I was afraid of unintended consequences to the family I had only begun to discover.

There was no putting the genie back in the bottle, though, and I had to accept that the news media was on the long list of things over which I had no control. Later that spring I joined hundreds of other pro-life people in Sioux City for the 40 Days for Life initiative. While praying in front of an abortion clinic I was approached by a woman who told me, "I know who your birth parents are. I went to high school with them. You should know that your birth mother had a great faith – she would talk about her religious beliefs long before it was 'cool' to do so." Another time I was shopping in Target when a stranger came up and said, "You're that abortion lady, aren't you? I knew your birth father!"

You knew my birth father? How I wish I could say the same!

In the spring of 2009 I was asked to speak at a pro-life dinner in Onawa, Iowa. While I was at the podium, I noticed a man in the audience struggling to fight back tears. I wondered what I had said that affected him so much and resolved to seek him out at the end of the program. I was amazed when he was invited up to the stage to give the benediction. He was a Catholic priest, and I'll never forget what he said, the tears still glistening in his eyes. "Who says prayers go unanswered?" he asked. "I used to pray outside St Luke's Hospital in 1977 that a child's life would be spared from abortion – and here she is!"

I couldn't believe my ears. After the event we spent some time talking, as Ryan, Olivia, my mom, and my aunts who had come to hear me speak circled around us. We hugged and thanked each other for speaking out, and as we parted ways we promised to pray for one another.

When I first started speaking out about being an abortion survivor, I saw it as a temporary, occasional activity. It was a way to make sense of what had happened to me – a "lemonade out of lemons" kind of experience. I was working through my own "stuff"; sharing it in public helped me do that.

But as time went on, my perspective shifted. Each time I spoke, I met people who had been directly hurt by abortion and who suffered in silence. I knew how it felt to be marginalized and stifled and disbelieved. It takes tremendous courage for women, and men, to share their abortion experience; each needs to do it in their own time, in a way that feels safe for them. I felt increasingly called to be a voice not for myself, but for others.

The first time I met another abortion survivor was in Ottawa, Ontario, where I had gone to speak at a youth dinner following Canada's March for Life. As I turned to leave the steps of a government building where I'd been listening to some singing, a young man walked up and whispered, "I'm one of you."

What was that supposed to mean? I was taken aback. "Do I know you?" I asked. "No," he replied. "But I know you are an abortion survivor. I am too."

He told me his story. Like me, he had been adopted as an infant. He only learned he had lived through an abortion when he met his birth mother at the age of twenty. She told him everything. He turned around to show me the back of his head, which was flattened from what he had been told was a partial-birth abortion procedure.

I have met many other survivors since. Among them are brave men and women who struggle with physical and emotional handicaps, including missing limbs and learning disabilities. Most do not want anyone to know their difficult stories; few have medical records, like I do, to prove they survived an abortion.

I had a feeling of solidarity with the other abortion survivors I met, but my heart really broke for the mothers who told me how much they regretted their abortions. Becoming a mother myself had helped me understand the depth of their anguish and loss. After each encounter I have offered a silent prayer for my own birth mother, asking for her healing and peace, and hoping she will know she is forgiven.

I received an e-mail one day from a woman who wrote that she had had an abortion at St. Luke's in 1977. She thought I might be her child, because she was sure she had heard her baby cry after the abortion procedure. She had read about me in a flier distributed in her church and tracked me down. I had to tell her that I wasn't her child, but we kept in touch. Talking about what had happened and pouring out her sorrow to me helped her find healing. She later wrote, "[Melissa] was the very first person in thirty-three years whom I told. I was fifteen when I had the abortion, and it was the darkest secret, one that I was so ashamed of, which I thought I would take to the grave. I never thought I would ever tell anybody. Not my husband, not my children, absolutely no one knew – and Melissa forgave me."

In the years since, I have received many messages like hers from people who are grieving over a child lost to abortion, often hoping against hope that, like me, their child is alive. One woman was haunted by the memory of an abortion she was coerced into by her mother. She was five months pregnant at the time of the procedure and was convinced that she had heard her baby boy cry before he was taken away. She begged me to help her find him. Another woman wrote to me about being taken to Mexico by her mother at the age of eighteen for a saline abortion of the twin boys she was carrying. She was in labor for twenty-four hours before she delivered her dead babies. "For decades I sobbed every time I recalled what I did," she wrote.

Fathers, too, reach out to me to share their guilt and their grief, and each story I hear makes me wonder what my birth father went through. What if he had known about the abortion but not about my survival? Had he carried that burden his whole life until he received my letter?

One man wrote: "I am a post-abortion father who has lived with my involvement in abortion for the past thirty-plus years. I had no idea what effect the abortion would have on every part of my life. It was all kept a secret. I lived with the guilt and shame of what I had been involved in plus a lot of anxiousness, anxiety, and hidden anger inside of me that I just couldn't understand." This father shared with me a letter he had written to his lost child, asking for her forgiveness. "Although I breathed a sigh of relief at the time because it seemed to make things much less complicated for me, I have to live with what we did the rest of my life," he wrote. "How I wish that I would find out that *my* daughter was searching for her birth father."

Another post-abortive father, Eric Blackwell, told me how he struggled with guilt for nearly forty years after he and his wife, who was pregnant with their child at the time of their wedding, procured an abortion: "On the drive home my wife and I had our only discussion about the abortion. It was a one-sentence monologue in which my wife said that they were twin boys. . . . I cannot deny that I experienced a sense of relief knowing my wife was no longer pregnant and that we had 'gotten away with it.' However, that relief was never accompanied by release.

A part of me died with my sons and I would never be the same again."

Mahatma Gandhi once said, "Forgiveness is a virtue of the brave." But I think the truly brave are those who ask for forgiveness. We all need to be forgiven! Everywhere I went it seemed I met someone who was suffering because they desperately wanted to ask forgiveness from a child whose death from abortion they had somehow helped to cause. I came to understand that part of my mission was to be a voice of forgiveness to them.

Of course, my mission was also simply to personify the humanity of the aborted "fetus" – to show that the fetus is actually a baby. It meant so much to me to receive this message: "I don't know if you remember me, but you came to my school to speak about your story. I came up to you at the end crying, and it was because of you that I have my beautiful baby girl. . . . I want you to know that you saved a life. You were a voice for my little girl when she didn't have one."

By the summer of 2010, I was working full time in child welfare, caring for a toddler of my own, and traveling two or three times a month to speaking engagements around the country. I was grateful that organizations were willing to bring me into their communities to share my story. The response I received encouraged me to do more. What had started as a sideline was quickly becoming my primary mission.

It was clear to Ryan and me that something had to give. We began to talk, and especially to pray, about what to do. Should I stop accepting speaking engagements? Or should I quit my job and devote myself even more to sharing my story? Ryan was worried about our finances, and I was too, especially since our health insurance depended on my job. But every day I had to kiss Olivia goodbye at daycare tipped the scales a little more in favor of making a change.

Like always, I was looking for a sign to point us in the right direction. One came, in the guise of an invitation for Ryan, Olivia, and me to go on a two-week speaking tour of Australia. Neither Ryan nor I had ever traveled so far from home; the only trip I had ever taken outside the country was to Canada. I was determined to take advantage of this opportunity and secretly began planning the trip as a surprise for Ryan. I called his boss to request time off, then put in for my own vacation days. When that was arranged, I sprung it on Ryan, and he was thrilled. Everything was set until I got a call from Australia saying there had been a mistake – the trip would take three weeks, not two.

Ryan was able to take more vacation time, but I wasn't. I had used all my accrued leave. I went to my boss with my dilemma. She was sympathetic but clear. "We love you, Melissa, and support what you are doing 100 percent," she said. "But you can't do both."

She was right. Her words cut through months of indecision. I resigned and called Ryan. "I did it," I said. "I quit my job."

Ryan and I had "set out into the deep," relying on God's providence. We were anxious and excited at the same time. But when I picked Olivia up at daycare for the last time, my overwhelming feeling was of peace.

When we returned from Australia, I settled into a routine that revolved around our home. I worked with a speakers' bureau to book speaking engagements a few times a month and expanded my outreach through my website. But the focus of my life was caring for Olivia and being a wife to Ryan.

Later I came across an interview with *New York Times* columnist and author Anna Quindlen. She talked about the work/family balance with which so many women struggle and said, "When in doubt, choose the kids. There will be plenty of time later to choose the work." I had made my choice, with the support and encouragement of my husband, and didn't doubt it was the right one. The summer after I stopped working full time, the richest blessing of all came our way when we learned I was carrying our second child.

# Eleven

*There is no greater agony than bearing*
*an untold story within you.*
—Zora Neale Hurston

I SENSED FROM THE START that this baby was different from my first. My pregnancy test – at the doctor's office this time – came back negative. I was disappointed, but not surprised. I dropped three-year-old Olivia off early on a Monday morning for her first day of preschool and spent the rest of the morning at home feeling at loose ends, with no Olivia around to keep me company and no new baby on the way. Later that day, though, I got a call from the nurse in my doctor's office telling me that the blood test they had taken to confirm I wasn't pregnant showed that I was. "That almost never happens, Melissa," she said, and we both laughed at the happy surprise.

Ryan and I celebrated that night and then shared the news with Olivia. She became a big sister the moment she heard; to her, we were now a family of four. Her new brother or sister became an everyday part of her life. That a tiny child was growing in my womb was imperceptible to the naked eye, yet to Olivia it was as obvious as the nose on her face. How true it is that "through the eyes of a child we see the world as it ought to be"!

When I woke up a few days later with excruciating abdominal pain, we feared we had lost the baby to miscarriage. But a trip to the doctor and a quick ultrasound showed the pain was caused by the rupture of a benign ovarian cyst I didn't know I had. The doctor emphatically assured me that it posed absolutely no danger to the baby.

Still, my "spidey sense" kept telling me that something was not quite right. Ryan joked that the reason I felt different this time around was because the baby had his temperament – calm and easygoing – rather than my hard-charging type A personality. Mom told me I should stop worrying about the fact that I wasn't having morning sickness and be grateful! I had to admit she was right.

I was grateful, above all for the new life within me. I had a busy travel schedule that fall, speaking on behalf of pregnancy centers and pro-life ministries around the country. While I was away on a trip I noticed a small spot of blood on my underwear. I called my doctor back in Sioux City in a panic. "This can't be normal!" I said to the nurse who came to the phone, choking back the tears that were welling up in my throat. "Actually, Melissa," the nurse gently said, "it can be normal. You are only about six weeks along. She reassured me as best as she could, telling me that about 20 percent of women have some bleeding or spotting in the first twelve weeks of pregnancy. "Just take it easy and don't worry!" she urged as we hung up the phone.

About three weeks later, I had to leave town again. I was fast asleep in my hotel room in Warsaw, Indiana, after an event I had spoken at when I woke up in a cold sweat from an all-too-realistic dream. In it, I was having a miscarriage, and I cried out, "I don't know why this is happening!" I turned to see God sitting next to me, holding my hand, and he said, "You don't know yet, but I do. Don't be afraid." I tried not to let the dream shake me; I had experienced nightmares before, including when I was pregnant with Olivia. But deep down, I sensed that my dream was my mind telling me what my body already knew.

I flew from Indiana to Virginia, where I was scheduled to speak at a benefit for the Paul Stefan Foundation. This organization was founded by Randy and Evelyn James after the birth and death of their son. Paul Stefan had been diagnosed in utero with a hole in his diaphragm, which led to his organs being pulled into his chest cavity and his lung development being inhibited. This condition is always fatal, and the Jameses were urged to have an abortion. They refused, and in thanksgiving for his brief life – he lived only forty-one minutes after he was born – they established a home to provide a haven for women facing crisis pregnancies and their babies. The first mother they helped was a young woman who had been homeless; her baby boy was born one year to the day after Paul Stefan was.

My speech that night was as much for me as it was for the audience. It was about the importance of accepting God's will, whatever it is, and the beauty that unfolds when we do. I was so emotionally connected to Randy and Evelyn's loss, and to the amazing good that was now being done for women and children in need through their son's life. I prayed that I would have the same faith and trust if our child died.

The symptoms I had first experienced at around six weeks of pregnancy were still occurring now that I was nearly ten weeks along. My first appointment with my ob/gyn was scheduled for the following week. Because of my symptoms, and I think mostly because I was so obviously concerned about them, her office scheduled me for a sonogram the day before my appointment.

While I waited, I tried to keep my mind off my worries. We had a beautiful Indian summer that year, and we took advantage of it by spending as much time as possible outside. I'd take Olivia to the park after I picked her up from preschool and we would eat a picnic while watching the squirrels gather nuts for winter. At home, I tried to distract myself from worry by cleaning out closets and sorting through all the gifts I had been given by the sponsors of the speeches I had made around the country. In the pile I found a book printed with an image of Jesus and the words "I trust in you!" I wasn't familiar with the Catholic devotion to Divine Mercy that it represented, but I clung to the words to allay my growing fears.

Jesus, I trust in you! How easy it was for me to trust him when I was anticipating the arrival of a new baby – and how hard to trust his will when I feared our baby was in mortal danger. Ryan and I tried not to dwell on the what-ifs. Yet as we celebrated our sixth wedding anniversary two days before our ultrasound appointment, our thoughts were focused not on each other but on our hopes and fears for our unborn child.

I was eleven weeks pregnant on the day of our ultrasound. The technician had a kind yet professional demeanor, but I could see her concern as I described my symptoms to her. As she began the exam, I closed my eyes and offered a silent prayer that our child would live. When I opened them, I knew the answer. The images were projected onto a large, black television screen on the wall. We could clearly see that the gestational sac was empty. Our baby was gone. Our child would live in eternity, but would never be in my arms on earth.

The technician urged us to wait until the radiologist had reviewed the images, but I didn't need a radiologist to tell me what my body, and spirit, had been telling me for weeks. Although I had prepared myself for this moment, when it came the pain was more than I could bear. I felt like the Psalmist: "My tears have been my food day and night, while people say to me all day long, 'Where is your God?'" I never felt so far from God as I did after my miscarriage. He had given us a child, and I had lost it. I had failed Ryan. I had failed Olivia. Most of all I had failed my precious unborn baby, who had died in my womb.

"Was this pregnancy planned?" the doctor asked Ryan and me, as we sat in her office the morning after our ultrasound. It was supposed to have been our first prenatal appointment; instead, it was our last. I wasn't expecting the doctor's cold, clinical question; her nurse had been warm and consoling, and had confided that she, too, had lost a baby through miscarriage. I stared at the doctor through my tears, too stunned to ask her what difference it would make. Could she possibly think our pain would have been less if our child had been "unplanned"? Did she think I would be secretly relieved that our baby had died if I hadn't planned my pregnancy? I know doctors can sometimes become numb to death, but I recoiled at her callous assumptions.

The pain of her words was nothing, though, compared to what was to come. I went from her office that morning to the pre-op appointment for the S & C, suction and curettage. Those very words stirred up a feeling of revulsion in me – it was too close to an abortion. Physically, my body had been struggling without success to complete the miscarriage for weeks. Surgery was the only option. I told Ryan I could handle it by myself – I didn't want him to have to miss any more work. It wasn't going to be a big deal, just some paperwork, right?

Wrong. As I sat in the waiting room, it seemed that everywhere I looked I saw a mother with a newborn child, or a woman heavy with a healthy pregnancy. My eyes were drawn to them. Their very existence seemed like a cruel rebuke to me, yet I couldn't look away. I felt sorry for the medical clerk who greeted me that morning, who had to look at my tear-streaked, swollen face as I struggled to answer her routine questions and record my medical history. In the midst of that, my mind flashed to my birth mother, and other women who have had abortions. Do the doctors and staff they meet see their tears, or acknowledge their pain? How many enter a medical facility alone with no one to comfort them?

Paperwork done, the procedure was scheduled for the next day. I went home in a state of shock. My rational self knew that miscarriage is a common occurrence, an outcome for which I was not responsible. But my heart and soul felt a heavy burden of blame. I hadn't been able to protect my baby; my body had failed him and he had died. Ryan comforted me as best he could. He told me later how helpless he felt: "I couldn't do anything to help you or make things better. I couldn't bring our baby back. Men are supposed to protect women and children. And I hadn't done it. I couldn't do it."

I know Ryan grieved for our baby. But no man can understand the depth of the pain a woman experiences when she loses a child. With heavy hearts we both went to tell our little daughter that the baby she couldn't wait to meet would never be coming home.

I stayed up all night praying that somehow my miscarriage would complete itself naturally, so surgery could be avoided. I couldn't stand the thought of them taking what was left of our child, even though I knew his tiny body was already gone.

The next morning, as Ryan and I sat in my room at the surgery center, I felt numb and detached from all that was happening around me. I had never had surgery before, so I was a little scared of the unknown. As the anesthesiologist asked me what the surgery was for, I felt like screaming out loud, "What do you think it is for? Can't you see?"

I never felt so alone as I did when I had to leave Ryan behind and follow the nurse down the long hallway to the operating room. I started to cry and just couldn't stop. "I'm so sorry," I told the trio of nurses, as they prepped me for surgery. "It's just so painful. You know my baby is gone, don't you? This isn't what I wanted!"

"We know, honey, we're so sorry for you," the nurse closest to me said, as she began the IV drip. "Go ahead and cry – let it all out! You have a right to feel sad."

Every step I took down that hallway, every tear I shed as I lay on the operating table in the midst of my own pain, I couldn't stop thinking about the women who have abortions – and about the woman who had carried me. Even with all the love and support that I had from my husband, family, and friends, I still felt so alone, so scared. What had she felt?

><

In the days and weeks that followed, the sadness threatened at times to overtake me. No one knows what to say to you after a miscarriage. It was just as well, because I didn't want to talk to anybody. Like the Old Testament figure of Rachel weeping for her children, I could not be comforted, because my child was gone.

Even the sweetest of consolations felt bitter. Sleep eluded me. I would wander through the house at night, checking that the doors were locked and making sure that Olivia was breathing. Like any well-resting child, her breathing was so light that I could barely make it out from the doorway. I would approach her and lightly lay my hand on her chest in the hopes that I would feel its tiny heaves without waking her. I pressed my ear close to her lips to feel her warm, slumber-rich breath.

Years later, I read that "a miscarriage is the loss of a child who is just as real and has just as much value as any other child of any age." That's how it felt to me. Ryan's patient and steadfast love sustained me, as did Olivia's innocent and openhearted acceptance of our loss. After collapsing into bed early one morning after a sleepless night, I had a vivid dream of my baby being cradled in the arms of an angel. In my dream I heard a voice tell me that we had a son in heaven, and his name was Gabriel.

Gabriel – the name means "God is my strength." Relying on my own resources, I had faltered. But now, when I thought of the child I had lost, I would be reminded of the source of all strength. I knew in that instant that even though my arms were empty, the purpose of my motherhood had been fulfilled. Gabriel's short time in my womb had led him to eternal life.

As time went by, we all began to heal. As so often is the case, a little child led the way in banishing our sorrow. One day a few months after my miscarriage, Olivia turned to me and said, "You know, Mommy, the day Gabriel was born was the best day of my life!"

I gasped. What did she mean? She was barely four years old. Had she misunderstood what happened all along? Turning to her, I said, "Honey, you know that Gabriel wasn't born. You know that he died inside me."

She put her hands on her little hips and admonished me. "Mommy, he was too born! The day that he was made is the day he was born – and when I say it was the best day in my life, I mean it!"

Children are so wise. Her brother became a person the moment he was conceived, and Olivia understood that.

She was right: we now were a family of four because the spirit of our son would always live with us. God healed our grieving hearts and left in them the fruit of peace. We stopped longing for and seeking another child and began to trust in whatever plans God had for us – even if that plan meant the family we had so hoped would grow in size was now complete.

Not long after we lost our son, I came across a remarkable book titled *Letters to Gabriel.* It was written by Karen Santorum, the wife of Senator Rick Santorum of Pennsylvania, who was at the time crisscrossing Iowa in a bid for the Republican presidential nomination. The book was a compilation of letters she had written several years before to her son, who developed a life-threatening birth defect and died from complications of intrauterine surgery undertaken to correct it.

Reading *Letters to Gabriel* was cathartic for me – I wept over almost every page. But as usual, it was the poetry that moved me most.

And I heard a cry
That of a mother weeping
for the child
that was no more
And the wail echoed
across the mountain peaks
of her agony
And it sounded
down the years
it seemed
to all eternity

It was a cry
of such utterable pain
and grief
from a mother's
shattered heart . . .

(quoted by Santorum from *At the Death of a Child,*
by Donald L. Deffner)

I felt a deep solidarity with women everywhere who have
lost a child in any way. Whether our child died through
illness or accident, abortion or miscarriage, we share an
unspoken bond of sorrow.

# Twelve

*A ship is always safe at the shore –*
*but that is not what it is built for.*
—Albert Einstein

THE EXPERIENCE OF LOSING Gabriel brought me closer in my mind and heart to the woman who had carried me. I had thought of her all my life. As a teen my feelings toward her had been dominated by anger and confusion. Later, my search for her had been driven by curiosity. Those feelings had long since been swept away. In their place were compassion, understanding, forgiveness, and love. Olivia's birth had united us as mothers; Gabriel's death had united us in loss. My grief was searing; how much more had she endured? I wondered if I would ever know.

I hadn't heard anything from my birth mother's family since the letter I had received from her parents in 2007.

I still didn't know her married name or where she lived. My one avenue to contact her had been closed off by her parents' refusal to pass my letter along to her. The only way I knew to reach her was through the speeches and interviews I gave. I used every opportunity to say the words I most wanted her to hear: I forgive you.

Telling my story brought me into contact with another person from my past, one I never knew existed. I had established a Facebook page to reach out to other abortion survivors and support my work as a public speaker. In March 2012, I received a message saying, "Melissa, were you cared for at the University of Iowa hospital? If so, then I believe I rocked you as a volunteer. I distinctly remember a tiny infant with the same story in 1977 or 1978."

I sent an instant reply: "I did, Michelle! Oh my gosh . . . Here I am at the airport, crying . . . Thank you for helping to love me into life!"

Thirty-four years earlier, Michelle had been a nineteen-year-old volunteer in the neonatal nursery while she studied to be a pediatric nurse. She loved giving TLC to the tiny babies when their families couldn't be there. She told me about the day she looked around the nursery and saw that all the babies were asleep. "Too bad!" she had said to the nurse in charge. "No one to rock today!"

"Not so!" was the response. "Sleeping babies need love too!"

Michelle randomly picked a baby; she remembered my silky, jet-black hair. Starting to rock, she cheerfully asked the nurse, "What's this little girl's name?"

"She doesn't have a name. She's up for adoption; she was aborted but survived. We call her Katie Rose."

Michelle never forgot that day. As she put it, "God burned your image into my brain!" Now we were talking and planning to meet again after all these years. Between battling illness, traveling, speaking, and home responsibilities, several weeks passed and we still hadn't managed to get together. On April 12, I had to head out to Sedalia, Missouri, to speak to the Vitae Foundation, a national pro-life group. On my way, I received an e-mail from my contact at Vitae. It read, "We just found out yesterday that a lady who is attending our event was volunteering at the hospital after you were born. She says she held you." Apparently Michelle lived near Sedalia and had learned I would be speaking there; she was coming that night to meet me.

It was overwhelming to meet someone who had cared for me long before I myself understood what I'd been through. How glad I was to be able to publicly thank her for remembering me, in a world that would rather forget lives like mine. Like Mary, the nurse who had cared for me in Iowa City and had become a lifelong friend, Michelle is a great blessing in my life.

Every four years, my home state of Iowa is overtaken by political fever as candidates from both parties vie to win the nation's first presidential nominating contest. Despite my early interest in politics, I had avoided getting caught up in the process. But in August 2011, before I knew I was pregnant with Gabriel, my mom, Olivia, and I attended the presidential straw poll in Ames. This event is a cross between a county fair and a political convention. All the candidates show up to make their pitch to the crowd and entice them with food and musical performances before a straw poll is taken to determine the early favorites. It's an exciting, entertaining spectacle, and we all enjoyed it. As we were leaving, I spotted a bus emblazoned with the emblem of the Susan B. Anthony List. I admired their work to elect pro-life women in both parties to political office, so I stopped by to say hello. Mallory Quigley, their communications director, recognized me from a video of a speech I had given and introduced herself. We exchanged contact information and I felt I had made a new friend.

After listening to the candidates I decided to support Senator Rick Santorum for the nomination. Why him? Well, I admired his integrity and legislative record. I had been comforted by his wife's book telling the story of the life and death of their son Gabriel. Most of all I wanted to support him because he had led the fight in the US Congress for legislation to ban partial-birth abortion, a method in which a late-term baby is killed by scissors stabbed into its soft skull moments before its head is delivered. Before it was banned, the method was routinely used to abort babies in the seventh month of gestation. Had this horrible technique been used by my abortionist, I would not have survived.

I followed the campaign closely, and in February 2012 I made my way to West High School in Sioux City to stand up and be counted for Senator Santorum. He won a narrow victory in Iowa, but went on to lose the Republican nomination to former governor Mitt Romney of Massachusetts. Still, I had been bitten by the political bug, and wanted to stay involved in my home state.

The following summer, I got a call from one of Mallory's colleagues at the Susan B. Anthony List, inviting me to join a bus tour around Iowa in support of local pro-life candidates. I felt so energized by the people who gathered to hear what I had to say, and by the SBA List team, that the long trip seemed worthwhile. The bus, however, was a little less energized – it broke down and the whole crew piled in my SUV to make the trip to our next stop in Mason City!

It was fun and rewarding to be taking a political stand in my home state. I certainly didn't expect that just a week later, Mallory would call to ask me to take a stand on a national stage. SBA List wanted to highlight President Obama's opposition to legislation to protect infants born alive after an abortion. My story dovetailed with their message. They asked if I would tell my story in a national ad campaign that they hoped to air during the fall campaign.

In my mind, I said, "No way!" But somehow out of my lips came the words, "OK . . . I'm listening . . . I'll think about it." As I thought about it, I realized that I had other commitments that would make it hard for me to go to Washington to film a political ad. I was scheduled to be in Tampa at the end of August to give a speech to a subset of the Republican National Committee, after which I was taking Olivia on a long-promised trip to the "magical kingdom" of Disney World. I called Mallory to gracefully bow out, only to learn that the ad would be shot in Orlando – right on our way.

Gulp.

Left with no plausible excuse, I agreed to do the ad. I met with SBA List's ad team in Florida and we quickly completed our work. The text of the ad read as follows:

I was aborted, and my body discarded . . . like I didn't exist.

But a nurse heard me crying . . . and cared enough to save my life.

There's something else you may not know: When he was in the Illinois State Senate, Barack Obama voted to deny basic constitutional protections for babies born alive from a failed abortion. Not once, but four times.

I know that it is by the grace of God I am alive today . . . if only to ask America this question:

Is this the kind of leadership that will move us forward? Leadership that would discard the least and the weakest among us?

The ad was slated to run in several key states, starting with a slot during the Democratic National Convention coverage in early September. I may have been a political neophyte, but I knew airing my story during the convention would invite a response. However, I wasn't prepared for the ferocity with which I was attacked.

Within days of the ad appearing online, the *Washington Post* called me a liar, saying I couldn't prove my words that I had been left to die. My appearance was mocked by a sneering commentator who called me "Crazy Eyes." I was even more rattled by people who took to Facebook and other social media platforms to mock and denounce me and question my honesty. Yet for every attack that came my way, there were many more messages of support and encouragement from people who were moved by my story.

As the attacks mounted, I felt a grip of fear around my throat, the same fear that earlier in my life had kept me from giving witness to the truth of my existence. The folks at the SBA List were thrilled with the response – to them all press was good press, and the fact that people were writing about the ad, even to attack it, was proof of its effectiveness. I couldn't be so detached. It was *me* they were talking about: *my* appearance and demeanor, *my* integrity and truthfulness!

My fears intensified and threatened to take me back to a very dark place in my life, one I had mercifully escaped with God's grace as a teen. I poured out my anxiety to Ryan, who reassured me that I had nothing to fear. He took practical steps, like changing my passwords and increasing security settings on the internet and social media. By helping me focus on the things I could control, he helped me deal with the things over which I had no power, like the opinions of others.

A few days after the ad began to air, I traveled to Georgia for a speaking engagement to benefit a pregnancy center. I felt beaten down by the attacks from outside, but even worse was the fear within. It seemed like everything had spiraled out of control. As I made my way to the banquet hall and waited to be introduced, I struggled to push away my racing thoughts and keep my mind on the message I was to deliver. The woman who was to introduce me stepped to the podium. Her words calmed my nerves and lightened my spirit. She told how inspired she and the staff, volunteers, and board of the center had been by the SBA List ad, and how fervently they had been praying for me to receive the grace of God as I stepped forward with my story in the midst of a presidential campaign.

When I returned to my hotel room that night, I was at peace. I awoke the next morning feeling renewed and confident. No, I wasn't in control. But God was.

Mom and Olivia came with me to DC later that fall to participate in some events sponsored by the SBA List.

I'll never forget Olivia's face the first time she saw the ad air on the television in our hotel room in Virginia. She couldn't fathom how she could see me on a television screen and standing in front of her at the same time! I got how surreal it was for her, because it was surreal for me too. How had I managed to get myself in the middle of a presidential campaign? It was a little frightening to realize how far I had put myself "out there," not knowing how my story would be used and if it would have an impact.

My foray into electoral politics was a brief one. We moved from Iowa to Missouri in 2013, so I can't even participate in the famous Iowa presidential caucus. But I don't regret my experiences during the 2012 campaign. In 2011 one of my favorite singers, Kelly Clarkson, released her song "Stronger." It's a song of lost love, which thankfully doesn't apply to me. But when I look back on that time and the anger behind the attacks made against me for standing up for the unborn, its lyrics come to mind:

> You think you got the best of me
> Think you've had the last laugh
> Bet you think that everything good is gone
> Think you left me broken down . . .
> Baby you don't know me, cause you're dead wrong
> What doesn't kill you makes you stronger
> Stand a little taller . . .
> What doesn't kill you makes a fighter
> Footsteps even lighter.

I am a stronger voice for the unborn because of what I endured during the 2012 campaign. And I am committed to using that voice behind the scenes and in front of the cameras to speak up for the babies who have been silenced and the mothers who have been deceived by a culture of death that convinces them that the price of their happiness is the life of their child.

# Thirteen

*Secrets have a way of making themselves felt,*
*even before you know there's a secret.*
—Jean Ferris, *Once Upon a Marigold*

I EXPECTED AN ORDINARY DAY as I relaxed on the couch one beautiful morning in March with my second cup of coffee. I had just dropped Olivia off at preschool and had set aside a stretch of time to work my way through a full inbox. I often heard from people who had heard my story and wanted to connect. I had met wonderful people this way and gotten a few surprises as well – like Michelle, the nurse who had held me as a newborn. But nothing could have prepared me for the message I clicked open that morning.

"Dear Melissa," it read, "I've been wondering whether to write to you or not for over 3 years now, although I have thought about you for much longer than that. I asked my first cousin – your birth mother – if it would be all right if I contacted you." I let out a cry of shock, and steeled myself to keep reading. The writer went on to imply that there was more to my story than what I was sharing on my website and in my public speeches. "I was around 14 when you were born in Sioux City and I have a perspective on the whole situation that you may want to explore. . . . If you would like to contact me, I would be happy to get to know you."

What a mix of emotions I felt on reading this message! My first reaction was to be defensive and a little apprehensive – if there was something I didn't know about my story, it wasn't because I hadn't tried to find out! At the same time, I was deeply grateful that this cousin, whose name is Susan, was willing to reach out at all. More than anything, I felt hope: a door to my birth mother, which I'd feared was closed forever, had cracked open.

I answered Susan right away, and as we exchanged e-mails I shared the documents I had acquired and told her everything I had discovered in my long search for the truth.

Over the following days and weeks, Susan included some other family members in our exchange, including my half-sister Jennifer. That took some getting used to! Jennifer was just a few years younger than I was, a married woman with children of her own. It was surreal after such a long search to now be exchanging e-mails with a biological sister. And although her main focus at first was to open a channel of communication between me and her – our! – mother, over time we developed a friendship that became one of the great blessings of my life.

With each e-mail I learned a little more about the story of my birth mother's life. Some of it confirmed things I already knew from Grandpa Don and my birth father's family, or had surmised. Susan and Jennifer described my mother at the time of my birth as a vivacious, intelligent girl, in love with the boy she had been dating for years and planned to marry. The girl and her boyfriend graduated from high school and went off to different colleges. They got engaged and he gave her a ring; she was wearing it in early 1977 when I was conceived.

Throughout her spring semester and the summer that followed, my birth mother was blissfully unaware of her pregnancy. She had always had irregular periods and didn't notice anything was amiss. She had been training intensively as a member of her college volleyball team and was eating a restricted diet, so didn't gain any weight. It wasn't until she was home over the summer that she put on a few pounds, and even then, she didn't attribute it to pregnancy. Then on a Sunday in late August, shortly before she was due to return for her sophomore year of college, her mother approached her with an abrupt demand: "Let me feel your stomach." It was only then that my mother learned she was carrying a child.

My mother was stunned and confused, but her mother, an experienced nurse, was swift and decisive. My birth father was summoned to my mother's home.

When he arrived, he was told my mother was pregnant. My mother's siblings were ordered out of the house, but my grandmother's angry voice could be heard through the windows and doors. She made it clear that abortion was the one and only option on the table, and that an end to my parents' relationship – something she had sought since the accident nearly two years before – was non-negotiable. That evening was the last time my birth parents were in the same room; they spoke, but never saw one another again.

That conversation took place on Sunday night, August 21; by Wednesday morning, August 24, the saline abortion had begun.

➴

I remember with vivid clarity the moment I read the next words in the e-mail: "The abortion was against your mother's wishes." I sat in stunned silence, and then began to weep. I had met so many women who had endured what had happened to her; I knew the pain they carried every day. Like so many women whose pregnancies are inconvenient to people around them who are more powerful, my mother was forced to have an abortion. One telling detail gave me a glimpse into what she had been up against: Susan wrote that my grandmother had made my mother sell her engagement ring to help pay the medical bill for the abortion.

My heart ached for this young girl, afraid and alone, forced against her will – by people who should have protected her – to end the life of her child. But as I wept for her, I felt a private joy for myself: I had been wanted, and loved, after all!

What the e-mails told me next, though, was almost more than I could bear: While I was fighting for my life in the NICU, my mother's parents told her I had died. She never consented to the adoption that was arranged behind her back. I tried to grasp what my relatives were telling me: For most of my life, my mother had thought me dead!

I had walked through the looking glass – like Alice in Wonderland, I felt like I "knew who I was this morning, but I've changed a few times since then." The facts of my birth were the same, but the context had completely changed.

My mother had not known I existed; she didn't find out I had survived the abortion until after my letter to her parents in 2007. She had not even seen the medical records related to her hospitalization and abortion, the records documenting the efforts made to end my life, and my improbable survival, until I shared them with her. All the years I had searched for those records to verify my story, I never dreamed that their greatest value would be to reveal to my mother the details of what had happened to her.

Amid all these stunning revelations, one inconsequential question passed along from my birth mother touched me in an unexpected way. She is left-handed and wanted to know if I was too. (I'm not.) I had always hoped to find a physical resemblance between us; to realize that, naturally, she would have the same desire sure gave me a lot of hope.

Ryan was the only person in whom I confided what I was learning from my birth mother's family, but the stress of telling my "old" story in public while keeping my "new" story secret began to get to me. Ryan was worried and encouraged me to take things slow. He didn't want me to get hurt. I was plagued by anxieties I thought I had overcome long ago and developed shingles, something that had happened before in times of great stress. One day I shared with Susan what I was going through.

Susan replied with a message forwarded directly from my birth mother, saying I should publicly share the truth I had learned. She said: "I need you to keep speaking. You are the first person to ever fight for me."

It took a minute for the words to sink in. She saw my work as an advocate for the unborn and against the violence of abortion as a way of fighting for her! What a beautiful way of seeing things, an insight I knew had to be the fruit of deep pain. It expressed so clearly the truth that a woman can never really be separated from her baby; the violence of abortion is directed against both the child and its mother. I can't begin to express how much those words meant. My mother knew I cared. We were on the same side. Through me, her story could be told.

That story included one final secret that chilled me to the bone. One Sunday morning, I noticed a new e-mail from my half-sister Jennifer. We had been corresponding for several months and had shared much about our lives. I had come to look forward to her messages, so I opened her e-mail eagerly although I was still in bed.

Both Susan and Jennifer had hinted earlier that there was something they weren't telling me – something it might be better not to know. Jennifer's e-mail that Sunday morning revealed this secret. I realized immediately why they had hesitated; it was something I never could have suspected. My medical records include this line: "The baby was delivered spontaneously in bed by a nurse." Jennifer now told me that our grandmother, a nurse, had been in the room – she had assisted in her own daughter's abortion! When I was born alive, she not only concealed that fact from my mother, but demanded that I be left to die. The brave nurses who defied her saved my life by rushing me to the NICU, where the fact of my survival couldn't be denied. But they couldn't help my mother, left alone with the grief her own mother had inflicted.

I had heard many shocking secrets since I first sat with Mom all those years ago in our Storm Lake living room and learned I had survived an abortion. But nothing could have prepared me for this. I was devastated. Olivia heard my sobs. She climbed onto the bed and wrapped her arms around me, eyes wide with concern. How could I ever tell her that someone to whom she was biologically related could have committed such a cruel act? I wanted to put my head back under the covers and stay there, but something – or Someone – beckoned me out that morning.

Ever since the man in the parking lot of Sioux City Planned Parenthood had put a rosary in my hands all those years before, I had been led, slowly but inexorably, to the Catholic Church. I had resisted at first, but ultimately my defenses crumbled. Ryan, Olivia, and I had moved to Kansas City, Missouri, earlier that year, 2013, to take advantage of job opportunities for Ryan. It had been hard to leave our home and our many friends in Sioux City. It had had been our home for ten years, the place where we had fallen in love and become a family. Moving away meant no more breakfasts at the diner with Grandpa Don, no more easy drives to visit our families in Iowa. But in our new home, after years of feeling disconnected from my own church, and encouraged by the faith and witness of so many Catholics I had met through my years of speaking out, I started attending Mass at the parish in our new neighborhood. I knew right away it was where I belonged; it felt like coming home. I started formal instruction in the faith shortly thereafter.

It was to this church I turned the Sunday morning I learned my grandmother had delivered me and left me to die. I tried to understand what could have motivated her. Had she thought she was doing what was best for her daughter? Had she really thought her daughter's welfare could be purchased through the death of her first grandchild? Or was she trying to protect her own image? I would never be able to ask her in this life; she was already dead. I found myself pitying this grandmother I would never know. Pity, though, isn't the same as forgiveness, and I knew I must forgive. But how could I? She had wreaked havoc not only with my life but with my mother's as well. Weren't some things beyond forgiveness?

As we rose to say the Lord's Prayer, my eyes were drawn up to the crucifix over the altar, to Jesus dying on the cross for my sins. ". . . And forgive us our trespasses, as we forgive those who trespass against us. . . ." I knew Jesus was giving me the answer. I had no choice: I had to forgive! I left Mass that morning still sad, still unable to understand what had driven my grandmother to do what she did, but at peace.

⊰

On August 29, 2013, I celebrated my thirty-sixth birthday. I marveled at how things had changed over the past year. We lived in a new city. I was part of a new church. I had learned more about my improbable beginnings. Some of what I'd learned was extremely painful, but much of it filled me with joy and hope. I attended Mass that morning and looked forward to celebrating later in the day with Ryan and Olivia. What I didn't expect, but was overjoyed to receive, was a birthday greeting from my half-sister Jennifer, flowers from my cousin Susan, and, most unexpectedly, an e-mail from my birth mother.

"Dear Melissa," she wrote, "Thirty-six years ago I was robbed of you. How I wish things could have been different."

How can I ever describe how I felt when I read those words? All those years I had wondered what role she had played in what had happened to me, always believing she was culpable in some way. Now I knew that she had been a victim, too, and was just as traumatized as I had been by the awful truth. I had waited decades for the day when I could celebrate my birthday knowing something about the woman who had carried me toward that fateful day in 1977. Now I knew a truth that was far different from what I had expected – more tragic, but more hopeful too. I felt a strange intermingling of sadness for both of us over what we had lost, and anticipation of what might come in the future.

In that e-mail exchange, and many others since, we shared the things we had only pondered in our hearts. She told me of her joy when she found out that I had lived, and of her feelings of loss and betrayal when she discovered the circumstances. She told me how proud she was of me, how sad she was that she had been robbed of me, and how she couldn't believe I could love and forgive her. She told me how happy she was that I had been adopted into a loving home, and asked me to thank my mom and dad for giving me their love and support, and for teaching me well.

At long last, my story was her story too.

# Fourteen

*The life of every man is a diary in which*
*he means to write one story, and writes another;*
*and his humblest hour is when he compares the volume*
*as it is with what he vowed to make it.*
—J. M. Barrie, *The Little Minister*

By the time Christmas arrived in December 2013, my birth mother and I were in tentative but regular contact. We exchanged holiday greetings and gifts. I sent her a photo album filled with pictures from my childhood; Jennifer sent me an e-mail the next day saying it "made" her mom's Christmas. I had something else to share with my birth mother and her family that Christmas too, for just a few weeks earlier Ryan and I had learned I was pregnant.

We had been trying without success to conceive another child for many months. The disappointment was hard to bear, especially coming as it did after my miscarriage. I was thirty-six years old – the ticking of my biological clock sounded like a time bomb! I had resigned myself to the possibility that we would never have another child, but when I started to feel queasy in the early days of December, I secretly took an at-home pregnancy test. I didn't feel like I was pregnant and didn't want to get Ryan's hopes up. The positive result was a sweet and welcome surprise.

One of the shocks of having a baby after the age of thirty-five is learning that the medical professional considers you old. My "advanced maternal age" earned me a referral at twenty weeks to a maternal fetal health center for genetic counseling and a more sensitive ultrasound.

Ryan and I had no intention of subjecting our baby to prenatal genetic testing. The process of amniocentesis – sticking a needle into the womb to withdraw amniotic fluid for testing – can cause miscarriage, and nothing we could learn from it would change the fact that our baby was a child of God, and of ours, unconditionally loved no matter what.

We were excited about the ultrasound, though, and thrilled to learn that we were having another girl. Olivia had been praying for a sister. That day she was sure God had answered her prayers.

It was Easter time, and I was about to be received formally into the Catholic Church. I was twenty-four weeks pregnant. How far I had come from the day I was confirmed at the Methodist church in Storm Lake! Now, God was knitting together in my womb a baby girl. Like St. John the Baptist in his mother Elizabeth's womb, our child leapt with joy when I received the Eucharist and the gifts of the Holy Spirit through confirmation that night. Not long after we decided on our daughter's name – Ava, which means "breath of life."

On Wednesday afternoon, August 6, 2014, a few minutes after one o'clock, she was born. She had a shock of dark hair, like mine, and Ryan and I immediately fell in love with all 7 pounds, 3 ounces of her. A few minutes later, Olivia was allowed to see her sister. I beamed with joy at my girls, knowing how long we had waited for this moment.

Within moments, though, our joy turned to fear as we were told that Ava needed to go to the NICU. Her breathing was raspy and uneven; she needed specialized care. As Ava was whisked away, Ryan ran out of the room after her. As frantic as I was with concern, there was something so beautiful in watching my husband rush out to stay with our daughter, to protect her. After what seemed like an eternity, I was able to join them.

I will never forget the first time I saw Ava in the Isolette, clutching Ryan's pointer finger. Over the next several days the neonatal doctors and nurses worked to diagnose what was wrong. They told us Ava had a condition I had never heard of before but now know to be quite common – laryngomalacia, otherwise known as floppy larynx. The cartilage in her larynx was not as hard as what is typical and so it flops in, creating difficulties in eating and breathing. They assured us she would grow out of it. On a blazing hot summer day, we left the hospital at last. I squinted in the bright sunshine after being inside for so long. Olivia beamed as she sat beside her baby sister. A short drive later, we were home.

Ava's first year was rocky – so much so that I felt I could write a companion to the bestselling book most new mothers consult; my book would be titled *What Not to Expect the First Year!* Because of the problems with her larynx and a cyst on her tongue that was diagnosed later, Ava had difficulty breathing and trouble drinking or holding down nourishment. Most days were an endless cycle of long, laborious feedings followed by violent bouts of throwing up. No matter what we tried, it seemed we could do nothing to soothe our fragile, vulnerable, hungry baby girl. It was heartbreaking to see her suffer and frightening to see her fail to grow and thrive as she should.

Ava endured one medical intervention after another, and after each one the high hopes we had were dashed. Doctors prescribed different medications and therapies. One terrifying episode sent her to the hospital in an ambulance in the middle of the night after a bout of reflux left her limp and struggling to breathe. Finally, after months of searching for a treatment to relieve her pain, in early December Ava was admitted to the hospital for surgery to repair her larynx. The surgery was a success but it led to the discovery that she had another complex condition that led to fluid from her gastrointestinal system collecting around her lungs. A chest tube was inserted to drain fluid from her lungs and a feeding tube to ensure she received nourishment while her body healed. This complication kept her in the hospital until just a few days before Christmas. We were so happy that we would be able to celebrate Ava's first Christmas at home with her big sister. We were hopeful that Ava's troubles were behind her.

But that was not to be. At home, Ava's breathing and feeding issues resurfaced, and two days later she was readmitted to the hospital after fluid was again discovered around her lungs. The day before Christmas dawned for Ava and me in the pediatric intensive care unit, separated from Ryan, who was home with Olivia. This wasn't how Christmas was supposed to be, and yet it turned into a special joy. All the superficialities were stripped away, and we were left with the essentials: our family, our faith, and our hope. I spent a few hours with Ryan and Olivia at home that night – one of only three times I left the hospital during Ava's stay. We opened gifts and received messages of love and support from our families, which now included not only my parents and Ryan's, but also Grandpa Don and Aunt Vicki, Jennifer and Susan and my birth mother. On Christmas Day, Olivia was able to visit Ava at the hospital. Ryan and I looked on as Olivia whispered softly to her sister and held her tiny hand. We were reminded of the true meaning of Christmas.

Ava was discharged from the hospital on New Year's Day. It felt like she, and I, had been reborn. She still faced difficulties and required a feeding tube for several months, but time and Ava's resilient spirit won out. When she uttered her first word at ten months – "Mama" – I melted. She started crawling at one year, and soon she was pulling herself up and cruising along the furniture. She walked at sixteen months, and by eighteen months she had caught up developmentally and was even advanced in some areas.

On a particularly rough day, I remember looking at Ava and wondering, "Who would you be if you weren't facing all these difficulties?" I heard back from the depths of my soul, "She would not be who she was created to be, just like you would not be who you are without your own struggles." As mothers, as parents, we want to protect our children from suffering, yet their happiness and destiny may well depend on the hardships they encounter. Ava without the issues she has faced would not be Ava. I'm grateful God trusted us enough to make her our child.

We hope the difficulties of Ava's harrowing first year are behind us now, with no lasting ill effects. But that experience opened my eyes to the crushing pressures faced by families whose children have complex medical needs. I can remember how it felt to be faced with the fear that our child might struggle or suffer her entire life. I remember what it's like to feel afraid and powerless in the face of my child's pain. My experience gives me a greater empathy for parents who might be tempted to choose abortion to avoid this fate. But I've seen firsthand the sunshine that comes after the storm for these children and their families. Ava has been a fighter, just like me, from day one. She brings joy to everyone she meets, and I can't wait to see what she accomplishes in her life. She is the strongest reminder of my mission: to tell whoever will hear that every child is a unique thought of God.

# Fifteen

*The world's favorite season is the spring.*
*All things seem possible in May.*
— Edwin Way Teale

AFTER A STRING of rainy and blustery days, the sun emerged from hiding on May 22, 2016, to shine on the kind of spring day that inspires poets to write odes of praise. Olivia and I had an outing planned – we were going to the zoo – and she had been counting down the days with great anticipation. We had almost cancelled earlier in the week when Ava had come down with a respiratory infection that landed her in the hospital overnight. But she was home and feeling much better.

As Ava slept blissfully under the watchful and loving gaze of Grandma Terry, Olivia and I scurried around the house getting dressed and packing up the car. Ryan hovered nearby; he had planned to stay home with Ava and his mom, but now was having second thoughts.

"I would love for you to come, Ryan, but don't feel you have to. I'm okay. I don't need to be protected," I assured him.

"I know that, Missy. I'm not going along to protect you. I just want to be with you and Olivia today."

Daddy's decision to join us made what was already a great adventure for Olivia and me even better. As we settled into the car to begin our trip, my mind went back to the second reading at Mass that morning from Paul's Letter to the Romans, about how "hope does not disappoint." What had started as a tiny seed of hope in my heart had now blossomed like the spring flowers all around us. Today was the day I would meet my birth mother.

We had inched toward this day over weeks and months and years of getting to know each other from afar, through notes, cards, and e-mails. Susan, my mother's cousin, had been a constant source of encouragement, always nudging us toward each other with love. Jennifer and I had forged a friendship that grew stronger with each text and e-mail. Yet after the date was finally set, Ava's sudden hospitalization had threatened to derail our plans. Her quick recovery cleared the last obstacle to a reunion that had been nearly thirty-nine years in the making.

Why had it taken so long? I don't know the answer, but I have come to believe that God's time is ordered always to our happiness. The prospect of meeting my birth mother face to face would have frightened me just a few years earlier. I would have tied myself in knots: What to say? What to wear? What if it doesn't go well? What will she think of me? But today I only felt gratitude and peace – a peace born of the many baby steps that had led us to this moment, each one guided by God's gentle, loving hand.

Still, as Ryan, Olivia, and I sat watching the sea lions playfully thrash around their pool, a feeling of sheer panic started in the pit of my stomach, urging me to flee. At that moment, my phone buzzed beside me. The text message was from my half-sister, Jennifer. "We're here!" she wrote. "Where are you?" Ryan and I looked at each other for a long moment, took Olivia by the hand, and stepped out toward the picnic area about a hundred yards away where we had planned to meet. I didn't see them at first, but then they caught a glimpse of us and started waving. We quickened our pace and they came into focus. They were holding hands, and as I approached I saw Jennifer drop her mom's hand. In an instant I was enfolded in the arms of the woman who had carried me.

We hugged for a long time – so much love and pain, hope and forgiveness were communicated in that embrace.

"I can't believe this is really happening," she said.

"It has been a long time," I replied.

With tears streaming down all our faces, we made our introductions. I hugged Jennifer as my birth mother hugged Olivia and Ryan. Jennifer had brought her two children, one a tall and willowy girl about Olivia's age. They became fast friends – cousins – without a moment's hesitation, as if they looked at each other and recognized a kinship. Jennifer's little boy was a quiet redhead with a gentle demeanor who was about the same age our Gabriel would have been had he lived.

The kids led the way – Olivia and her cousin walking hand in hand, amused by the animals they saw. The adults shared in their fun, and in a deeper joy of mutual discovery. I hadn't expected how comfortable – how right – it would seem for us to be together. We talked of things large and small, and laughed much more than we cried. But the tears did flow as my birth mother and I spoke for the first time of what had led us to this glorious, improbable day.

I remarked to her with a smile that I was sure she had realized long ago that I looked like my birth father.

"Yes, you do," she said, "but when I show my friends and coworkers pictures of you, they say you look like me from the nose up."

"You show my picture to people?" I asked.

"Of course! I keep the photo album you sent me for Christmas a few years ago in my car, and show people the pictures all the time. I keep a copy of your medical records that you sent to me there too, just in case someone says they don't believe what happened to us."

I can't begin to put into words what it meant to me to hear her say that she saw herself in me, that she shared our story with her friends, and that she offered the proof of our history to anyone who doubted the truth. As a child I had spent endless hours dreaming of how I might look like my birth mother. Later, after I first saw her photo, I struggled to see the resemblance. Now I recognized a connection that went far beyond any superficialities of appearance.

The questions about my birth that had once dominated my mind seemed to fade in importance. Our meeting was more than I could have hoped for. But the things I learned from her that day were everything I ever suspected, and worse. I was filled with grief for the pain and sorrow she had endured.

"My greatest regret, Melissa, is that I didn't just run away," she said. She told me that her parents were outraged by her pregnancy, ashamed about her being unmarried and pregnant, afraid of what it would mean for their reputation in the community. The most obvious solution – marriage – was the one her parents most opposed. They were adamant that their daughter not marry a man whose background and prospects were so modest, in their opinion. They were intent on their daughter making a "better," more socially prominent match.

In haste and secrecy, an abortion was arranged. My birth mother, feeling powerless and afraid, made clear that she did not want to go through with it. Her parents made clear to her that it wasn't her decision to make. "The procedure was horrible," she said, "but I was drugged and don't remember much."

What she did remember nearly broke my heart. Four days after the saline abortion began – less than a week after my mother had learned she was pregnant – her father brought her twin sister to St. Luke's to see her. While their father waited in the car, my mother's twin went inside and was directed by nurses to a private room on a quiet corridor. My mother was alone in the room, lying in bed tethered to an IV. Her sister, shocked to see her looking pale and semi-conscious, stroked her hair and softly whispered, "I'm scared." My mother replied by saying she was scared, too. Her sister asked her if the abortion was what she wanted. At that, my mother clearly replied, "Of course not. I never wanted this. I want to run away."

With her sister's help, my mother got out of the hospital bed. As the sisters tried to figure out how to make an escape, a nurse entered the room. She pushed my mother back into bed and turned to face her twin: "Just what do you think you are doing?" My mother's twin explained that my mother did not want an abortion and they were trying to leave. "If you take her out of the hospital now," the nurse said, "you'll kill her for sure. It's too late." My mother reached for her sister's hand, but the nurse separated them and sent my mother's twin into the hallway. Another nurse came and escorted her to the parking lot, where her father waited. The next day, I was born.

My birth mother continued, "After you were born, my mother told me not to look at the 'hideous' baby. I thought  it was because she was afraid I would be upset by a gruesome sight; I never dreamed it was because she didn't want me to see that you were alive. I was told emphatically that you were dead."

My birth mother left the hospital in a daze, unsure of how to put her life back together. She didn't go back to USD, but instead went to college in Sioux City. She grieved deeply over the abortion, but had no inkling I had lived until she got a call from her sister in 2007, shortly after I had sent my letter to her parents and had received their response.

"Are you sitting down?" her sister asked.

What emotions she felt when she learned the truth of my survival! Rage at being lied to, yet joy that I had somehow lived! It was in that moment that she learned for the first time that her baby had been a girl. Now she shared with her daughters the news that they had a sister. Yet she waited to reach out to me, unsure of what to say, afraid of how she would be received, certain I would never believe that she did not know I had lived.

The biggest mystery – how I could have been adopted without my birth mother's consent – was solved, Jennifer told me, when she finally got from her grandfather the records he had kept about my birth. In a manila envelope labeled "The 1977 Incident" were copies of the adoption consent forms. When Jennifer showed her mother, she said her signature had been forged. A comparison with other signed documents from the time period soon confirmed this.

How could anyone make sense of a betrayal like this? In my birth mother's case, the first casualty was trust – in her parents, her siblings, in doctors, in God. "I believe everything happens for a reason," she told me, "but where was God back in 1977 when I needed him?"

"I understand how you can feel that way," I said. "I have a hard time trusting, too. But I hope you will come to believe that God is with us right here and now, in this moment, as I do."

We shared many confidences that day, but our greatest joy was just being in each other's company. My birth mother asked about my parents, wanting to express her gratitude to them for giving me a happy home, a loving family, and constant love and support. She hoped they would be happy that we met.

"I know I will never be 'Mom' to you, but I just hope I can be in your life," she said before we parted.

"Yes, absolutely, I want that too," I said. "There's no rule book for this, but I know we can find a way to be a part of each other's lives from now on."

As we hugged goodbye, our spirits were light and our plan was to meet again soon. I felt as if a great weight – one I hadn't even been fully conscious of – had been lifted from my shoulders. Ryan had been a quiet presence all day – close at hand but giving me and my birth mother and sister the space we needed. Now he gave me a willing ear as I tried to process what had happened, and a peaceful silence when I wanted to ponder it in my heart.

🙚

The month of May – when we celebrate mothers of all kinds – had brought a great gift of healing and hope to me and to the woman who carried me. As I thought about the violence that had been done to my birth mother and to me, I recalled a passage from Genesis: "You intended to harm me, but God intended it for good to accomplish what is now being done, the saving of many lives."

# Sixteen

*Don't you think it's rather nice to think that we're in*
*a book that God's writing? If I were writing the book, I*
*might make mistakes. But God knows how to make the*
*story end just right – in the way that's best for us.*
—E. Nesbit, *The Railway Children*

ABOUT A YEAR after Ava's birth, I received a letter
from the Judiciary Committee of the United States House
of Representatives, inviting me to testify on Capitol
Hill at a hearing to consider ending federal funding for
Planned Parenthood. It was one of the greatest honors
of my life to be invited to tell my story to the nation in
the halls of Congress. What made it even more rewarding was that sitting beside me, telling her story too, was
Gianna Jessen, the abortion survivor I had seen on television when I was a teenager and who had helped me
realize I was not alone. Gianna and I met for the first time

that day, and we offered our testimony on behalf of survivors everywhere. "We are your friend, your coworker,
your neighbor, and you would likely never guess just by
looking at us that we survived what we did," I testified.

Life has led me places I never would have chosen to
go, and yet I clearly see God's design as I look back. I
was devastated when I found out I had survived an abortion. My first reaction was fear, followed by anger that
I turned on myself. I felt guilty about my own survival
and ashamed of who I was. God's grace transformed my
anger to grief, for myself and for the woman who had
carried me. For me, grief led to forgiveness, and its fruit
has been love. There was a time when I was afraid of the
unknown, paralyzed by anxiety. I tried to control what
I could rather than face what I could not. That time has
passed. I don't hide my scars anymore, but wear them
proudly, for they are a sign that God heals.

Once, I sought contact with my birth family so I could
get answers to my questions. Now my only desire is that
they know I love them and that they are forgiven.

I love the lyrics of Don Henley's song "The Heart of
the Matter."

> I've been trying to get down
> to the heart of the matter.
> Because the flesh will get weak
> and the ashes will scatter.
> So I'm thinking about forgiveness . . .

Forgiveness really is the heart of the matter. Forgiveness toward the people who tried to take my life before I was born and toward the people who have mocked me or called me a liar through the years – we must "bear with one another and forgive" as we have been forgiven. Forgiveness eases our pain and gives us peace.

Meeting my birth mother and her family was the beginning of what we both hope will be a relationship that grows and deepens over the rest of our lives. I know how fortunate I am to even know who the members of my birth family are, much less to be in touch with them. So many adoptees search their whole lives in vain. So many women who have had abortions would give anything to know that somehow their child had lived. I am humbled and grateful.

Many people think abortion is a discrete act that has no lasting effect. They are so wrong! Abortion can't be compartmentalized and is never forgotten. And its effects ripple through generations.

I recently read something singer Stevie Nicks said in an interview in 1992. Speaking of her four abortions she said, "To give up four babies is to give up a lot that would be here now. So that bothers me, a lot, and really breaks my heart. But they're gone, so . . ." Years later she confirmed that her song "Sara" was written in part for one of those babies (whose father was Don Henley, writer of the song I cited above about forgiveness). I've heard an echo of these lyrics in the voices of every woman I have met who regrets her abortion:

> Sara, you're the poet in my heart
> Never change, never stop
> And now it's gone . . .
> All I ever wanted
> Was to know that you were dreaming.
> (There's a heartbeat
> And it never really died.)

I realize my situation is uncommon: I survived abortion with no permanent physical or emotional handicaps. I've grappled with questions about why my life was spared when millions of others died. As well as to be the unique person I am, including being a wife to Ryan and mother to our children, I'm convinced God protected me to be a voice for the voiceless – and their mothers.

My life has been a roller coaster of highs and lows with barely a moment to catch my breath in between. What's important, though, isn't the ride, but the destination, and the people who come alongside you on the way. I don't know what the future holds, but I do know, as John Henry Newman once said, "God has created me to do him some definite service. He has committed some work to me which he has not committed to another. . . . I am a link in a chain, a bond of connection between persons. He has not created me for naught. . . . Whatever, wherever I am, I can never be thrown away."

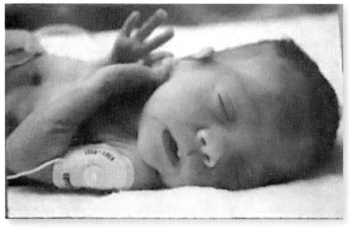

I'm twenty-five days old.

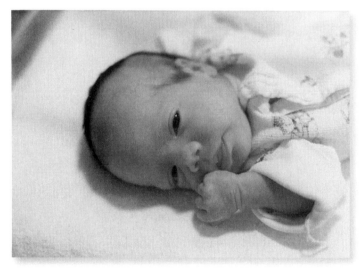

As I looked when Mom and Dad saw me first, at one and a half months.

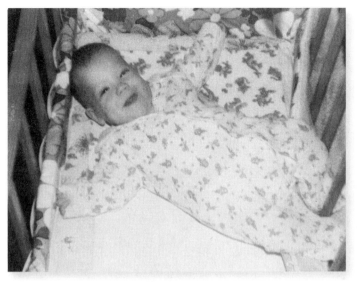

Already thriving at five months old.

Horseplay with Dad. I'm about to turn one and Tammy is just about five.

With Mom and Laddie outside our home in Curlew, Iowa.

Christmas, a little later that same year, 1978.

Mom and me in the garden. I'm two.

Tammy and me—best friends at this point.

Those were happy years with not a care in the world.

Here I am when I started school in 1983, and then at fifteen,
in ninth grade.

Two photos from 1996, the year I graduated from high school.

Ryan and I are engaged, 2005.

Our first child, Olivia, arrives April 2008 at St. Luke's Hospital, where I was born.

Family time during Ava's difficult first year, February 2015.

Ava at eleven months, at her first ballgame.

Olivia and Ava, love perfected.

# Acknowledgments

THERE ARE SO many people who have been a part of the story of my life to whom I owe a debt of gratitude.

My birth mother and father, who conceived me in love; my parents, Ron and Linda Cross, who gave me everything when I had nothing; my siblings, Tammy and Dustin, and all of my grandparents, aunts, uncles, cousins and friends who gave me their unconditional love and support.

I owe special thanks to my birth mother for sharing her own story with me, reviewing my manuscript and contributing additional details, and encouraging me to share our story with the world. And I will always be grateful for my birth father's aunt, Vicki, who was the first to welcome me to his family, and to Grandpa Don, who loved and accepted me and made sure I knew I was not a secret to be hidden but a blessing to be shouted from the rooftops! I am thankful, too, for my birth mother's cousin Susan, and my half-sisters Jennifer and Sarah. We have walked through the dark together, and emerged into the light. I look forward to the rest of our story.

Ryan is the solid foundation upon which our whole lives are built. I couldn't make it through one day without his love and that of our daughters Olivia and Ava, and our son Gabriel in heaven.

I am grateful for my editors, Sam Hine and Mary Cannon, and the team at Plough for all they have done to make this book possible.

Above all, I owe a debt I can never repay to Jesus Christ, my Lord and Redeemer, and to his Blessed Mother Mary, who tenderly cares for all mothers and their babies.

MELISSA OHDEN IS founder of the Abortion Survivors Network and an advocate for women, men, and children impacted by abortion. With a master's degree in social work, she has worked in the fields of substance abuse, mental health, domestic violence, and child welfare.

*melissaohden.com*


For a group discussion guide and other resources, visit

*youcarriedmebook.com*